Herbert Metford Thompson

The Purse and the Conscience

An attempt to show the connection between economics and ethics

Herbert Metford Thompson

The Purse and the Conscience
An attempt to show the connection between economics and ethics

ISBN/EAN: 9783337034573

Printed in Europe, USA, Canada, Australia, Japan

Cover: Foto ©Suzi / pixelio.de

More available books at **www.hansebooks.com**

THE
PURSE AND THE CONSCIENCE.

THE

PURSE AND THE CONSCIENCE

AN ATTEMPT TO SHOW THE CONNECTION

BETWEEN

ECONOMICS AND ETHICS

BY

HERBERT M. THOMPSON, B.A.

LONDON

SWAN SONNENSCHEIN & CO.

PATERNOSTER SQUARE

1891

PREFATORY NOTE.

A SUBJECT involving the consideration of some
parts of two sciences necessarily touches on
many points. The connection of these with
the main thread of argument in this little book
will not I think be lost sight of, if the reader
keeps the syllabus before him ; it is intended
to serve as a map.

The portions of the quoted passages on pages
45 and 147 which are italicised are so empha-
sised by myself, not by the writers from whom
the quotations are made.

I have been much indebted to Mr. Carveth
Read, who was good enough to read these
papers in manuscript and to suggest many
improvements in them.

H. M. T.

SYLLABUS.

INTRODUCTORY -   -   -   -   -   - page I

The attention aroused by poverty. Evils intense and
extensive resulting from it (1)—The specialists
who devote themselves to the subject are fully as
attentive to the latter as to the former. But the
sympathy and interest of the general public is
more easily aroused by the former (3)—This widely extended wish to do good to the poor founds
itself on different conceptions of the facts of the case,
and follows various methods (4)—These papers
endeavour to investigate what the real conditions
with which we have to grapple are, and what
methods of amelioration can be adopted with
security that they are well founded. They deal
with the connection between Ethics and Economics. This subject plainly in the first place
includes the observance of *Justice* in monetary
affairs (6)—Consideration of the meaning of
" Justice " in this connection. Different conceptions of justice in the distribution of wealth.

The idea is involved of a distribution proportionate to services rendered to the community. But
who is to assess the value of such services? (7)—
And must their reward be enjoyed solely by the individuals who have rendered them? (13)—The
following chapters attempt to unravel these questions. But as our subject is the connection of ethics
with economics, we are not bounded by considerations of strict justice merely ; nor are we
concerned to define very rigidly what justice is,
for, however wide we may make our definition,
the boundaries so set up will not be large enough
to include all ethical considerations. These will
step over such limits and enter the region that
lies beyond—that of generosity (14).

mechanical processes; fashion, and consequent
changes in demand for particular commodities.
Hence arises scope for ethical action (41)—
To make the system in any way complete there remain
on the community the duties of rendering the environment of the competitive system such that it
may work freely and fairly. This entails the
necessity of :—*(a.)* Suppression of crime. *(b.)*
Provision of health for those who would otherwise be crippled for the want of it. *(c.)* Provision of education for those who would otherwise
be crippled for want of the mental equipment
necessary in a complicated social system (42)—
We have had occasion to draw a distinction between
tendencies and accomplished processes in economic matters, and we have seen how ethical considerations are concerned in making allowance
for the intermediate stages, how, too, they are
further concerned in the necessity of perfecting
the environment and conditions of the competitive
system. Are the older economists right in thinking that when due allowance has been made for
these two sets of considerations, ethics will have
no further part in the matter, since satisfactory
results will be automatically secured by the
action of the competitive system ? (43)- -

Our Duty in relation to various existing Circumstances which tend to modify, and in some cases to nullify, the Justice with which Services to the Community are rewarded under the Competitive System.

Some of the modifying or disturbing causes are partially removable. Under this head we may include :—*(a)* Bad laws and bad customs sanctioned by law (51)—[Opposed by political organisations.] *(b)* Fluctuations in the value of gold and of silver (55)—[Remedy possibly not yet found.] *(c)* Ill-disbursed "charity" (63)—[Charity Organisation Societies.]

Others require reform rather than removal. *(d)* The poor law and the bankruptcy systems (65)—[Possibility of a more satisfactory life for paupers. Dishonesty and fraud should not, because they end in bankruptcy, go unpunished.] *(e)* Monopolies (68)—[Difficult to maintain for long together by means of combination. Possibly sometimes best met by legislation.] *(f)* Custom (71)—[Each custom must be considered on its own merits.]

The subject we now approach requires not reform but complete removal; but an alteration of ethical standards is first necessary. Full consideration

xiv   .   *SYLLABUS.*

of *(g)* Commercial immorality (73)—The commercial code of honour. [What our attitude should be towards—Bad work and adulteration(75) —Immoral and useless business(76)—Commercial bribery (77)—Deception (78)—The effect that chivalrous honesty in commercial affairs would have.] Lastly, and in a measure inclusive of the rest, we have *(h)* Wealth inherited irrespectively of services rendered to community by inheritor (83)— Hereditary wealth, moreover, perpetuates results of *a, b, c, d, e, f,* and *g,* and often of crime, infirmity, and ignorance also. [Possibility of increasing the scope of the " Death Duties."]

Taking into consideration the importance of the disturbing causes enumerated, it is no matter for surprise if we find that the unevenness of wealth-distribution is often not in accordance with the deserts of individuals (84).

CHAPTER III.—*Socialism* -   -   -   -   - 86

Resumé.—In Chapter I., ethical action was shown to be necessary in relation to the competitive system to free it from hindrances within and without. In Chapter II. ethical action was shown to be necessary in relation to other economic forces. In Chapter IV. ethical action

will be shown to be necessary to counteract the
ill effects of evils at present irremovable. May
all these difficult courses be superseded by the
short-cut of Soc'alism ? (86)—

Definitions of Communism and of Socialism (89)—

As the evils complained of are not inherent in competition, the *primâ-facie* case for its abolition is
weak (94)—Two reasons for thinking that the
proposed remedy is inadmissible :—

1. The competitive system *at present* the most powerful available impetus to the due fulfilment of
services to the community.

2. The competitive system, as far as I can see, *always*
will be the only test of whether given work is required by the community or not (95)—

1.

Supposed cases of the social motive, often the individualistic motive in disguise. Examination in
this relation of Co-operation (96)—Profit-sharing (97)—Of socialism itself (98)
Would not the abolition of competition intensify the
evil of the overcrowding of certain industries ? A
negative answer counts for nothing if given on
account o the degradation of the people—a

degradation removable by the fulfilment of the
ethical duties enumerated in Chapters I., II., and
IV. (103)—Examination of the proposal to pay
those whose work is required to carry on an industry a " fair wage " (105)—Abnormally low
wages the result of immobility of labour. Keeping this fact in mind, what would be the result of
the " fair wage" proposals ? (107)—" Fair wage "
for all applicants inadmissible (108)—" Fair
wage " for a chosen number of applicants im-
practicable. It would tend to force the residuum
downwards into lower and still more crowded
grades of industry, instead of making some
(it may be inadequate) place for them by tempting upwards the most competent (108)—The
idealists say that the social impetus ought to
tempt upwards as powerfully as the individualistic. True it ought to do so, but AS YET it does
not (111)—Still, why should not those to whom
it *is* as strong a motive act accordingly ? Most
certainly they will do well to do so, but do not
let them take for granted that it is *generally*
operative,—*e.g.*, do not take for granted that the
entrepreneurs as a class will feel the impulse of
the socialistic motive (112)—or that the individual
workman will in general do the best work of
which he is capable, if this impulse is alone relied

on(114)—The new impulse must become operative before we cease to rely on the old. Self-abnegation very easy to practise for individuals without assuming that it is the universal impulse (115)— But if Socialism is inadmissible, how comes it about that we already have much successful legislation that is accounted "socialistic," and contemplate more? (116) — Examination from this point of view of—The Poor Law ; (117)— the Factory Acts; (120)—the Post Office; (122)— Free Education (123)—

2.

Examples of the difficulty of measuring the extent to which certain work is demanded by the community, compared with other work, when we no longer have the test of competition to guide us (125)—Before abolishing the competitive system we must provide ourselves with some other automatic measure of the necessity of any given work (128).

Taking it for granted that the ill effects resulting from the imperfect working of the Competitive System (consequent on the faulty nature of its environment, and on various disturbing causes [considered in Chapter II.] co-existent with it) are

b

not likely immediately, or perhaps ever, entirely to be removed or reformed, what courses of action are desirable as tending to do away with such ill effects?

First. Self-denial with regard to luxuries (130)—Definition of luxury (130)—Leisure a luxury (131)—Self-denial with regard to luxuries should be practised because a smaller consumption by self gives the power of allowing to others a larger consumption (131)—The subject confused by the wage-fund theory and the deductions from it (132)—By relinquishing the wage-fund theory we are deprived of one argument for the limitation of luxury, but it was an argument that attempted to prove too much (134)—In reality the main reason for limitation of our own luxuries is that we may be able to attend to the necessities of others (135)—Are there solidly based ethical grounds for the preferring of investment to the luxurious spending of wealth? Investment implies the postponement of spending. Postponement always carries with it *chances* of less luxurious expenditure (135)—But if these chances do not take effect the advantages are most insignificant (136)—The conclusion is that the choice lies between :—(1) Spending on self. (2) Spending altruistically. And (3) Postponing spending, in which case we shall at a future time be again confronted with the choice between (1) and (2) but with a *larger amount* involved, the increase being the interest on the money which has accrued in the interval (140)—Putting bounds to luxury, is therefore not enough ; it is merely the first step which puts us in a position for altruistic expenditure (141)—

[*Parenthetical Note* on accurate comprehension of the real significance of conduct in economic affairs. Popular judgment in this respect often much astray (142)—Examination of particular cases. Papering a room with bank-notes (143) Making a present to the nation for the reduction of the national debt (144)—Gambling (144)— First and third class railway travelling contrasted (145)—Money spent in the encouragement of art] (148)—

Second. Discouragement of a disproportionate love of possession (149)—

Third. Recognition of our responsibility towards others in the regulation of our own money affairs (150)—The morals of investment. Investments which " pay on the average."

Fourth. Combating the social power of wealth.
Mr. H. Spencer on this subject (155)—The
principal difficulty is, that if wealthy men are
not conciliated, they may not use their wealth
in desired ways (160)—We must avoid allowing
the treatment of wealthy men to be distinc-
tive (162)—

In the application of ethics to economics, formulated thought is needful, but it should go hand
in hand with discriminating generosity and imagination (163)—
These papers urge the extension of ethics to
economics ; they do not suggest that economics
furnish the whole field for ethical action (165).

THE PURSE AND THE CONSCIENCE.

INTRODUCTORY.

THOSE who are outside the direct pressure of being obliged to face for themselves the problems of distress and misery arising from poverty, are often occupied with them in their thoughts. Callousness on the subject is not characteristic of our time; many of the pleasures of life are shadowed by a sombre consciousness of trouble not far distant, though perhaps unseen.

And indeed the subject is impressive enough whether we regard the intensity of the evils —overcrowding (inconvenient and unhealthy always, but terrible when there is a savage or drunken head of the family, or when fever or death are present), lack of proper food, shelter,

and warmth, filthy conditions of life, merciless
compulsion to ceaseless work,—or whether we
consider the extensiveness of the milder forms
of the miseries of which these are the severe
instances—the monotony, the dreariness, the
lack of interest surrounding so many lives; the
mediocrity which results.

Some years ago, on the occasion of a royal
visit to Liverpool, it was proposed that the
Prince's procession should go through a poor
part of the city; the suggestion provoked a
protest from one of the local newspapers; a
special reporter was sent to describe the district
and show how unsuitable it was that a Prince
should be asked to traverse it.   The first street
he visits he describes as "one in which fashion
"and beauty would be out of place," of the
next road on the proposed route he says, "a
"more gloomy view than that which will first
"meet their" (*i.e.*, the Royal Party's) "eyes it

"would be hard to imagine in a great city"
. . . "the vistas of which the royal visitors
"will catch a glimpse will not add to their enjoy-
"ment." He goes on to speak of the dingy,
crowded, smelling streets, "the normal ap-
"pearance of which is certainly most repulsive."
Thus some of the evils resulting from poverty
are intense, some are extensive. We notice
too that of the thought and endeavour directed
towards their removal some is intense, some
extensive.

The intense thought is applied perhaps
principally to the extensive evils; statis-
ticians watch phenomena and register facts
which enable political economists to formulate
theories concerning the causes of poverty, and
their best remedies; legislators and social re-
formers are thus furnished with some ground
for action.

But extensive sympathy is certainly most

easily excited by intense evils, and beyond those
whose lives are devoted to grappling with the
problems of poverty, we have a far extending
interest in anything that is popularly recognised
to have a direct bearing on the subject.   When
an endeavour is made to paint the picture of
poverty in unusually vivid colours there is a
quick response of interest, and without any such
special appeals being made, a continued
endeavour of some sort or other is always
going on " to do good to the poor."

But whilst we may acknowledge so much
bond of union in the thought and in the deeds
of many tender-hearted people, chaotic confusion exists in many of their minds concerning
points which are fundamental if such thought
and action are to be effective, confusion firstly as
to facts, secondly as to methods.

The only facts that appear to be established
are that poverty exists, and that wretchedness

results from it. If we ask further questions there is no unanimity in the answers. Are people poor by their own fault? or are they poor because they are robbed by the rich? or is it a mixture of the two?

Again, if people are poor by their own fault, does that make it any the less incumbent on the rich to help them? and most important of all, *can* the rich help them? Is poverty remediable by altering the social conditions of life? or is it dependent on individual character?

In method there is equal diversity. One good man gives bread to every one that asks at his door ; another starts a penny-bank ; another founds scholarships for penurious students. Some people devote their time to bazaars, some are enthusiastic about land-reform, some about trade-unionism. There is diversity between the somewhat unenergetic methods of the acquiescer in things as they are, and the often ill-balanced courses of the man who is in constant revolt against existent conditions.

This little book has been written in advocacy of facing differences of opinion concerning the facts of the problems of poverty, and the methods of grappling with them, and of endeavouring to discover which are right.

It is an attempt to make more clear for what part of their poverty the poor are, and for what part of it they are not, responsible; it considers the attitude of mind of the well-to-do towards poverty arising from each of these causes; it discusses, from the ethical standpoint, various aspects of the question of the distribution of wealth, and points of conduct and habit having to do with money affairs. It in fact deals with the connection between two sciences, that of Economics (the Science of Wealth), and that of Ethics (the Science of Right and Wrong); it accordingly attempts to show when and how

in monetary affairs questions of right and wrong
are involved.

They are in the first place clearly involved
to the extent that *justice* is concerned in distribution of wealth. But what is meant by a
just distribution of wealth? It may be defined
to be such a distribution as is proportional to
services rendered to the community. But this
definition is a wide one, and admits of various
interpretations ; we are at once faced with the
question, Who is to determine the worth of a
service rendered to the community? Is it to
be estimated by the average opinion of the
community at large ? Such an assessment may
be said to be carried out under the competitive
system, where the more a service, or a material
object resulting from work or from any other
service, is valued, the higher price or reward it
commands.

Sometimes however individuals thrust aside

this public assessment, and reward what appears to them to be merit, on a scale different to that which the play of supply and demand shows to be in force with the community at large. When for example princes have patronised the arts, they have often paid more than their market value for pictures, statues, or operas. Such departures from market-prices are made by those who believe that they possess exceptional judgment or enlightenment, and .presumably with the idea, that the world in general will with further progress endorse them as being in the direction of justice.

Other departures have been made and are still being made from those rewards of service settled by the average opinion of the community as shown by the effective demand, or by the price which will be generally given for a particular commodity. These departures are not made merely in anticipation of what a more enlightened public judgment may some day endorse, they are to a great extent irrespective of public judgment present or future.

Where wages and prices are fixed by custom and not by competition (as for instance is to a great extent the case in India) we have the most striking example of a distribution of wealth effected otherwise than by the public opinion of the community as shown in the play of supply and demand. Tradition is here powerful, and rewards for service which have once been adopted, become as it were crystallised. There is however reason to think that even here the laws of supply and demand do gradually make themselves felt, though changes that take generations or centuries to be consummated in India, might be brought about in a year or two in a highly organised commercial State. It is the flow of the glacier compared to the flow of the river.

In communities which are for the most part competitive the same phenomena are partially observable ; thus we had the mediæval attempts to fix by legislation the price of bread, the rate of interest, and the wages of labourers. The fixed tariffs of the old guilds have some counterpart in the "minimum wage" of the Trade-Unions of to-day, and the Socialists wish to carry the same methods of assessment very much further.

Of these modern instances it is especially observable that while there is a certain amount of *à priori* reasoning in the fixing of particular rewards for particular services (it is said for example that every able-bodied man *ought* to be able to earn enough to maintain himself and his family "in comfort"), the main lines of assessment are similar to those which govern what economists call normal wages and normal prices in the competitive community.[1] The difficulty of rendering the service is taken into account. Work that is arduous is to be rewarded more highly than that which is light, work that is difficult more highly than that which is easy. It asks of the worker, what strength of muscle, what power of brain does the service you propose to render, entail? Similarly of commodities, it inquires, is there here embodied much or little strength of body or of intellect?

In actual life we find that services to the

[1] Wages are normal when each wage-earner renders service to the community of a kind that is more valued than any other service he is (with equal endeavour) capable of rendering, and when each is paid the full amount the community will give rather than command other s rvices.

Prices of commodities are normal when no particular commodity is produced by endeavour or abstinence that would have been more highly rewarded if otherwise applied, and when for each commodity is paid the full amount the consumer would give for it rather than spend the amount on other commodities.

community of a particular kind (embodied perhaps in some particular commodity), are continually becoming more or less plentiful than
the wants of the community, *taken in conjunction
with all its other wants*, justify.   Under the
competitive system wages or prices then depart
from the normal level, they sink or they rise as
the case may be ; a special discouragement, or
a special encouragement, is thus extended to the
particular form of service in question, which
tends to decrease or increase its supply till the
normal level in regained.   The non-competitive
method of assessment complains of this as
unjust.   " *Why*," it asks, " should a woman in
" a match-factory be paid so much less than a
"shop-woman for work that is at least as
"arduous ? "   No inquiry is made concerning the
workwomen, as to whether there are many or
few who will perform this service and no other
for us.   There is neglect to inquire of a parti-

cular commodity, whether it is easy or whether it is difficult to get that particular embodiment of services (work and others) multiplied. Yet it is not difficult to show that as a particular form of service becomes disproportionally multiplied, it approaches more and more nearly to uselessness, and to anyone recognising a utilitarian standard of morality no injustice is involved in rewarding unequally work of like arduousness but unequal utility.

A point of greater difficulty is that though it is said that under the competitive system wages and prices continually *tend* to the normal, it is known as a matter of actual experience that in certain occupations and trades they never arrive at that bourn. Can it be said to be just that certain occupations shall be *chronically* underpaid ? This is a point which the following chapters examine with some care.

Another point of controversy arising from

our definition of a just distribution of wealth is, whether the reward of a service must be enjoyed solely by the individual who has rendered it, or whether justice allows him to transfer it during life or after death to other individuals?

It is plain then, that to determine what is a "just" distribution of wealth is a matter of great complexity, and in fact an unravelment of the difficulties thus presented involves an investigation of the problems this book considers.

Clearly it concerns ethics to determine at the least what in economic matters is, and what is not, just, but it is not incumbent on us here, I think, to pin ourselves down to any rigid definition of justice; for the field of ethics is wide enough to embrace generosity beyond the bounds of actual justice, and our investigation is that of the connection between economics and

ethics, between monetary affairs and considerations of right, irrespective of whether right be
involved in an attempt to be just, or in a more
extended attempt to be generous.

I.

How the Competitive System tends to award benefits in proportion to services rendered to the Community.

I ENDEAVOUR in the first part of this chapter (pages 16-26), very briefly to recapitulate the fundamental economic points which bear on our purpose. These of course are rendered familiar by the text-books, and an apology is perhaps needed for reiterating them here, but those who write speculatively on the ethical aspects of economics allow themselves such a large amount of freedom, that it has seemed to me advisable that we should remind ourselves on the threshold of the subject that the prices of services and commodities are not in the main fixed arbitrarily.

The Competitive System is in a wide sense a system of exchange resting in the first place on division of labour. If we suppose it possible for a State to exist in which each individual by his own unaided efforts produced exactly enough of the things that were required to satisfy his own wants, and those things of the precise kinds he required, if further he did not in any particular produce a superfluity above his own requirements, there could be no likelihood of the establishment of any system of exchange between individuals. But the division of labour places one set of advantages in the hands of one set of men, another in those of another, and some system under which they may barter amongst themselves becomes inevitable.

It is theoretically conceivable that all such advantages should be traceable to the results of labour or other services to the community

B

handed by gift, or transmitted by bequest, from one person to another. There is no inherent absurdity in supposing that even the private ownership in land might have originated in (as in fact the modern acquirement of land not unfrequently results from) individual industry. To maintain that the private ownership in land in this country originated and has survived as an equitable payment for services rendered to the community would no doubt be to strain unduly after what may be called historic justice, especially as the military services actually given were in the first instance rendered against those who at that time formed the community. But the fact that in the past landed and other property has resulted from violence and fraud, does not affect the conditions under which the advantages accruing from possession of such property may be bartered against other advantages in a state of society in which it is supposed that violence and fraud no longer hold a recognised place.

The competitive system then supposes a free exchange amongst individuals of the advantages which are their particular possession, whether such advantages result immediately from work, from work done by the individual in the past, from work the advantage derived from which has been transferred from others alive or dead, or from advantages transferred in the same way which owed their origin to violence, to fraud, or merely to good luck.

The greater the advantage an individual seeks to attain in an exchange, the greater will be the advantage he will be prepared to surrender, but it will be *his own* estimation of value in each case that will guide him.

Exchange then will only take place where each party to the transaction esteems what he is to receive more highly than what he is to part with. The number of bargains that can at any given moment be made in the world on these terms, though considerable, is limited, and would in time suffer exhaustion were it not that their number is constantly being recruited by specialised work.

The result of specialised work (and practically all work is specialised) is to accumulate in single hands, or sets of hands, advantages of the same kind more numerous than can be utilised to the full by their owners. Thus one man has the power of digging, and has the consequent advantage of having behind him every evening a well-ordered garden which lay before him in the morning untilled ; another man has the power of cutting coal in mines ; another that of writing business letters with rapidity and accuracy ; another that of making watches and clocks ; another that of organising commercial operations.

But any one of these will shortly produce more of his speciality than he himself desires to utilise, at any rate in proportion to his other needs. Let us take the clock-maker for example. The value to him of his clocks for his personal use falls as he goes on making more, and as the value of advantages resulting from other people's work remains as far as he is concerned constant, the conditions for bringing about an exchange are on his side ripe, that is to say, he esteems what he is to part with at less than what he is to receive. If a similar depreciation of property so far as they themselves are concerned takes place in the productions of the other workers, the conditions antecedent to exchange are perfected on both sides for several transactions in what we may suppose to be a little community.[1] Now, if the

[1] I am imagining a state of barter as showing the case more directly than if the intermediary of money is introduced,

community is one of very small size, all its members will very soon be supplied with time-pieces ; whilst the clock-maker has been making them, he has had his garden well cared for, his coal-cellar filled, his business letters written for him, and his money managed for him. The little circle now begin to order each a second clock or watch ; this, though possibly a convenience, is not nearly so valuable as the first. The gardener who has up to this time done as much for the clock-maker as for the collier, now begins to feel that the former can be less useful to him than the latter, and though he receives (in work) as much from the clock-maker as he did before, he gives him less in return. As time goes on and the clock-maker's work becomes more and more *de trop*, his position

but the principles under consideration are unaffected by the introduction of a standard of value as a medium of ex-change.

becomes worse and worse. This is because the community we have supposed is too small to support a clock-maker.

It usually happens however that communities are not so well supplied in proportion to their needs with the skilled work of the artizan as with the unskilled work of the labourer, so that in the experiences of actual life, it is more likely that we shall find the gardener than the watch-maker *de trop*, and in distress because his industry is "overcrowded."

At any given moment the demand for a commodity which results in acquirement by purchase is called the effective demand, and the amount of counter advantage which is bartered for the advantage arising from the possession of a commodity, may be called its price.

So far as men are influenced by the desire to barter their advantages on the best possible terms, they will tend to devote their energies to those kinds of work, the price of which is regulated by an effective demand more eager than the average, or in other words the price of which rewards the work more highly than other work that might have been done by the same individuals with an equal amount of effort.

Reverting to our example, if instead of imagining a small community we take the whole industrial system, we shall find that although the majority of mankind have more pressing needs than clocks to absorb their small incomes, yet, amongst those who are not the very poor, a certain proportion of what is spent they will wish to expend in clocks, at a price sufficiently tempting, when compared with the wages of other work, to induce men to enter the occupation of clock-maker. If we imagine the supply to be inadequate to the demand, the price rises, more young men are attracted into the field of occupation, and the supply becomes larger as the demand (in consequence of the enhanced price) becomes smaller. If on the contrary there are too many clock-makers for the demand, a converse process will theoretically take place.

Now the commodities, or the kinds of service for which there is the most eager effective demand (*i.e.*, the price of which is highest compared with that of other work that might have been done with equal effort by the same individuals), are those of which the community are in most need ; that is if we are prepared to accept the united judgment corporately expressed by the community of its own needs ; (in special instances we may think this much at fault—for example, the widely diffused preference for gin over classical music). Still, however much some of us may think our judgments wiser than those of the average of the community, we must admit that the latter is

entitled to much weight in such points as the
quantitative and relative desire for such things
as bread and beef, house-room and clothes—in
fact it would be difficult to measure the extent
of the need for certain services by the community in any other way than by examining
the amount of sacrifice it was prepared to make,
or counter-advantage to yield, in order to
command them.

But the kinds of service for which there is
most eager effective demand are also, as we have
observed, those which are most highly rewarded.   Hence it arises that there is a
proportion between the value of services
rendered to the community, and the reward of
such services.

The phenomenon which does more than anything else to obscure the operation of the
process, and the one which is most often cited
as confuting the accuracy of the theory, is the

inequality of reward of efforts that are equally arduous, and in a sense equally serviceable to the community. Thus we find a woman employed as a massage nurse earning perhaps 40s. or 50s. a week. We find other women doing work equally laborious in kitchen gardens at possibly 9s. a week. Not only do the women work equally hard, but, it is argued further, the kitchen-garden labourers do work that is as much wanted by the community. We should no more be willing to give up eating vegetables than we should be to do without the massage nurse.

The case here supposed is a repetition of that of the clock-maker in the small community, but, as we before remarked, it is usually the un-skilled, not the skilled work that is dispro-portionately plentiful. Thus in the case of the women garden-labourers, though it is true that a very large number might be engaged in the industry, and yet the effective demand for their work be so great that their labour would be rewarded proportionately well to other labour (of similar skill and arduousness), yet the number who actually enter its ranks is even greater, and their wages accordingly sink. The industry is, in fact, OVERCROWDED, that is, proportionately to other industries. It is without doubt possible to put one's finger on instances where it may be said with certainty that the amount of work and skill expended is less highly rewarded than the same amount of work and skill in some other departments of labour. The London needlewoman is an instance. How comes it about that this state of things does not right itself by the supposed automatic action of the competitive system, but that on the other hand it continues through generations ?

In examining how the competitive system puts right inequalities of remuneration, we have supposed that wherever work is paid more highly than the average the necessary number of additional workers are attracted into that field of occupation. This assumes what is called perfect "mobility" of labour; that it is available exactly where it is wanted, and immediately it is wanted. But as a matter of actual experience the difficulties encountered by those who endeavour that they themselves or their children shall enter into an employment far removed socially from the one they have been accustomed to, are so great that Cairnes, elaborating the expression of the same idea by J. S. Mill and others, divides work into certain groups of employments which he calls "non-"competing groups," regarding it as a moral impossibility for any considerable number of workers in one group to leave it for another where the conditions are more favourable.

"Of the disposable labour each element, that

"is to say each individual labourer, can only
"choose his employment within certain tolerably
"well-defined limits.   These limits are the limits
"set by the qualifications required for each
"branch of trade and the amount of preparation
"necessary for their acquisition.   Take an
"individual workman whose occupation is still
"undetermined, he will, according to circum-
"stances, have a narrower or wider field of
"choice; but in no case will this be co-extensive
"with the entire range of domestic industry.
"If he belongs to the class of agricultural
"labourers, all forms of mere unskilled labour
"are open to him, but beyond this he is
"practically shut out from competition.   The
"barrier is his social position and circum-
"stances, which render his education defective,
"while his means are too narrow to allow of
"his repairing the defect or of deferring the
"return upon his industry till he has qualified

"himself for a skilled occupation. Mounting a
"step higher in the industrial scale—to the
"artisan class, including with them the class of
"small dealers whose pecuniary position is
"much upon a par with artisans, here also
"within certain limits there is complete freedom
"of choice, but beyond a certain range practical
"exclusion ;" practically the man brought up to
be an ordinary carpenter or mason "has no
"power to compete in those higher departments
"of skilled labour for which a more elaborate
"education and larger training are necessary,
"for example, mechanical engineering." Similarly ascending a step higher, "persons com-
"petent to take part in any of the higher skilled
"industries" are practically excluded from the
professions. "It is true indeed that in none
"of these cases is the exclusion absolute. The
"limits imposed are not such as may not be
"overcome by extraordinary energy, self-denial,

"and enterprise ; and by virtue of these
" qualities individuals in all classes are escaping
" every day from the bounds of their original
" position." . . . . " But such exceptional
" phenomena do not affect the substantial truth
" of our position.   What we find, in effect, is
" not a whole population competing indiscrim-
"inately for all occupations, but a series of
"industrial layers superposed on one another,
" within each of which the various candidates
" for employment possess a real and effective
" power of selection, while those occupying the
" several strata are for all purposes of effective
" competition practically isolated from each
" other." . . . .   " No doubt the various ranks
" and classes fade into each other by im-
" perceptible gradations, and individuals from
" all classes are constantly passing up, or
" dropping down ; but, while this is so, it is
" nevertheless true that the average workman,

"from whatever rank he be taken, finds his "power of competition limited for practical "purposes to a certain range of occupations, "so that however high the rates of remunera- "tion in those which lie beyond may rise, he is "excluded from sharing them. We are thus "compelled to recognise the existence of non- "competing industrial groups as a feature of "our social economy." (Cairnes's " Leading Principles of Political Economy," Part I., Chapter III., § 5. See also Mill's "Political Economy," Book II., Chapter XIV., § 2.)

As illustrative of Cairnes's theory, contrast the monetary position of, shall we say, one of the most successful half-dozen barristers of our time, and of a man endowed with similar natural qualifications, but born into the labouring classes. Possibly his ambition will find its vent in becoming a leader in labour movements, but as for his wages, it is probable

c

enough that the hundreds of guineas received weekly by the barrister will have their counterpart in a corresponding number of hundred pence in the labourer's weekly incomings. Two main obstacles make it almost impossible that he shall become a successful barrister—want of capital, and following thereon, want of the needful education.

Prof. Francis A. Walker in his book on the "Wages Question" urges that Cairnes's conclusion should be somewhat modified, maintaining that the groups of industry are not so cut off from each other as he supposes. But on the other hand *within* the industrial groups depicted by Cairnes, Walker does not admit *as much* mobility of labour as Cairnes contemplates, pointing out that amongst the young people newly entering a trade (on whom Cairnes principally relies to adjust disturbances of the remuneratory balance), there is a very strong tendency simply to follow in their parent's foot-steps in the choice of occupation.

Putting aside for a moment any obstacles to entering a new occupation which are quite insuperable, the fact that one occupation is more highly remunerated than another makes it more *likely* that the workman will enter it because the inducement is greater; but we have to consider not only the inducement, but his susceptibility to the inducement—his adventurousness, pluck, refusal to allow his life to be wrecked through mere inertia.

These qualities, which we will describe shortly as "adaptability," influence the market value of labour just as the actual amount of labour or its skill does. But this fact does not disturb the correctness of the formula at the head of the chapter, that the competitive system tends to award benefits in proportion to services rendered to the community; adaptability is as genuine a condition of the rendering of service as industry itself or skill. This quality, like that of the mere fitness or ability for change of employment, as far as it is actually operative, finds under the competitive system free scope for beneficial action.

But if we recognise that industrious and skilful people are often underpaid because of lack of adaptability, it will suggest to our minds that to do what we can to increase their qualifications in this respect may in the long run be the best way of helping them to that " fair wage " which they only miss attaining for themselves by their lack in this particular. The worst of it is that adaptability (so far as it is the effect of character and not of environment), being the result of such things as good education, general intelligence, good information, versatility, and *savoir vivre*, the sort of pressure applied by the competitive system (the pressure of approaches by slow degrees to starvation), though it will often call forth industry, and sometimes skill, will seldom produce much effect in the particular direction indicated. Though it rewards the service when rendered, it does not make it appreciably more likely that it will be rendered. It is in fact just, but not educative. This is however merely saying that the competitive system requires supplementing by action suggested by ethical considerations ; in what particular ways we shall consider later. It is not an argument for that proposal (which we shall examine in a subsequent chapter—that on Socialism) to pay a fair or normal wage for all work done ; for though such a system may tend to increase the susceptibility to the inducement to enter over-paid employments, it removes the inducement itself.

It will be observed that the formula which

heads this chapter is not how the competitive system awards benefits, but how it *tends* to award benefits, in proportion to services rendered to the community. Probably many of the features which distinguish modern writings on Political Economy from those of the "Manchester School," are partly traceable to an appreciation of the important difference between a tendency, and a process which must necessarily be accomplished. It is curious that the late Prof. Fawcett, whose teachings in this particular we shall have occasion a little later in this chapter to criticise, should have emphatically insisted on the necessity of bearing in mind that the principles of political economy explain tendencies but do not necessarily proclaim results. The results he says depend on the balance of different political and social forces (" Political Economy," Book I., Chapter VII.)

The too abstract theory of Ricardo is true only of the " economic man," who, as Professor Walker says, " is taken as being perfectly cap- "able of judging of the comparative efficacy of " means to the end of wealth," . . . " that end " of wealth he never fails to desire with a " steady, uniform, constant passion " (" Political . Economy," Part I., § 20).

Later writers, whether English or American, have more and more regarded Political Economy as concerned with man as he *is*, as distin- guished from man as he theoretically might be. The economic forces whose play is thus newly brought into consideration are so numerous that positive prophecy can rarely be safe con- cerning the result of any one of them singly. It can merely be pointed out that certain tendencies will in time become operative if not counteracted by others.

Phenomena may be instanced where certain

results are ever in process of being consummated, but which nevertheless never attain to their consummation ; the older economists are apt to take for granted the perfecting of such results, their bent of thought being, that if it is not so now, we have only to wait a few years and it will be so. The newer economists see that this is making the same sort of mistake as an engineer would make if he assumed that every river source was at the sea-level, because water eventually finds its own level.

It is in some such way that we must account for the fact that all but comparatively recent economic writings ignore the economic phenomenon of different grades of employment, perhaps the very most important thing which those who concern themselves with such questions have to understand and explain. The old economists assumed as completely that it was a transient phase not requiring scientific investigation, as its permanent and unalterable nature was assumed by the framers of the Church Catechism when they were content to teach it as a precept, "to do my duty in that state of "life, unto which it shall please God to call " me."

An important hindrance to our being able to remove the word "tends" from the chapter-heading is found in the fact that there are rapid changes in the *sorts* of services required by the community, so that individuals who have qualified themselves to meet a distinct want are apt suddenly to find the conditions altered because the want no longer exists. One familiar instance of this is that of men's being thrown out of employment by the introduction of new mechanical processes.

Another is fashion. Prof. Alfred Marshall, speaking at the Industrial Remuneration Conference, 1885, said :—" Until a little while ago

" it was only the rich who could change their
" clothing at the capricious order of their dress-
" makers. But now all classes do it. The
" histories of the alpaca trade, of the lace trade,
" the straw-hat trade, the ribbon trade, and a
" multitude of others, tell of bursts of feverish
" activity alternating with deadening idleness.
" Everyone who changes the material of her
" dress simply at the bid of fashion sins
" against the spirit of art ; but she also
" probably adds to the wreck of human lives
" that is caused by the hungry pining for
" work." (*v*. The Report of the Industrial
Remuneration Conference, published by Cassell
& Co., Limited, page 176.)

Our theory must be further hedged about by
certain conditions under which it will alone be
free to operate. Of these the most important
are :—

(*a*) The suppression of crime and enforcement of contract and other legal obligations, by an efficient administration of justice.

(*b*) The provision of health for those who would otherwise be crippled for the want of it, by hospitals and the like (otherwise those who have failed in life, even though it be through their own inertness, will, if they chance to fall ill or meet with an accident, be *disproportionately* punished, for their chances of speedy recovery will be much diminished).

(*c*) The provision of education for those who would otherwise be crippled for want of the mental equipment necessary to success in a complicated social system. Of the kind of crippling that results from defective education we have already had an instance in the " non- " competing groups of industry."

The perfecting of these three conditions constitutes in the eyes of many the whole public social duty of man. They think that if these three duties are performed the competitive system leaves little to be desired, that anyone who did not prosper under it, would be found either not to conform himself to its regulations, or to be incompetent. Many of the foremost political economists, especially amongst the earlier writers, have adhered in the main to this idea. Even so recent a writer as the late Prof. Fawcett attributes inequality of wealth almost exclusively to the possession by some of more strength, ability, and industry, than others have, though he acknowledges the intensification of divergence where private property is inheritable. Thus he writes ("Political Economy," Seventh Edition, 1888, page 100):—

"Various schemes have been propounded "with the view of causing the wealth which is "produced to be distributed more equitably; "but if the State confiscated the property of "every individual in England to-morrow,

"accumulated the whole wealth of the country
"in one great fund, and divided all the land
"equally amongst the inhabitants, there would
"gradually arise the same inequalities of wealth
"which exist at the present time. *The in-*
"*dustrious would soon obtain those portions of*
"*wealth which were allotted in this national dis-*
"*tribution to those who were indolent and*
"*deficient in industrial capacity.* Men are
"differently endowed by nature, and those
"who possessed strength and ability would
"soon become wealthy, and those who were
"less strong and less able would quickly re-
"turn to comparative poverty." . . . . " These
"inequalities will be increased if a person is
"allowed to devise his property by will ; for a
" man who has already a great deal of property
"of his own, may have left to him the property
"possessed by four or five other wealthy in-
"dividuals."

A little later on (page 112) he writes:—

" There cannot be activity of trade without a
" keen desire for gain; but such a feeling
" indicates the spirit of competition, for in
" business men compete with each other with
" the view of securing the greatest possible
" gain. It is, however, important to present
" competition in a somewhat different aspect ;
" for the manner in which it has been here
" described may very possibly encourage the
" wide-spread error that with it there is
" associated something almost criminal. Many
" who profess to be social philosophers attach to
" competition the stigma of selfish greed. The
" poverty of the poor is often attributed to it;
" but we shall have reason to show that it is no
" enemy to the working classes. Without it
" their poverty would be rendered doubly
" severe; for it is an active spirit of com-
" petition which maintains the capital from

" which the labourers are paid." [Fawcett here
seems to make reference to the " Wage Fund
Theory," now abandoned by economists.]
" Competition befriends the working-classes in
" other respects; it cheapens commodities, and
" ensures that the maximum of wages shall
" always be paid. Competition is not confined
" to one class; it may be as rife among buyers
" as among sellers, or among the employers as
" among the employed. Individuals who have
" goods to sell are anxious to realise as large
" profits as possible; but when there is com-
" petition a trader cannot be paid more than
" what is termed a fair price for his goods,
" because if he attempts to obtain more than
" the ordinary price he will be undersold by
" other traders. When buyers compete with
" each other they are anxious to secure the
" greatest gains, or in other words, to buy
" upon the best possible terms; and thus, when

" buyers are each intent on purchasing on the
" most favourable terms, a commodity is sure
" to realise what it is worth.   It therefore
" follows that if on the one hand competition
" prevents a trader obtaining exceptionally high
" profits; on the other hand, it ensures to him a
" fair price for his goods.   Some, perhaps, may
" think it unfortunate that employers, stimulated
" by a desire to realise the largest gains, should
" seek to engage their labourers on the lowest
" possible terms.   But such conduct on the part
" of the employers inflicts no injury upon the
" labourers; for whenever there is activity of
" competition, an individual manufacturer or
" trader is as powerless to get labourers to work
" for him at less than the ordinary wages, as he
" would be to buy cotton at a cheaper rate than
" his fellow-manufacturers.   The price of cotton
" is maintained because there are those who are
" anxious to purchase it; the rate of wages is

" also maintained by those who are anxious to
" purchase labour. Competition consequently
" exerts no tendency to reduce profits or wages;
" the tendency is rather one of equalisation."

There is a touch of the grotesque about this
panegyric, for though the writer's contentions
might in the main be true in a state of free and
fair competition amongst " economic men," the
assumption that because competition is the
dominant note of present-day industry, every
failure in the balance of reward of merit will be
righted by automatic action, quite fails to take
account of qualifying considerations, however
important. Nor is the case altered because
most of the qualifying considerations may be
shown to be independent of, if not opposed to,
the competitive system—for the attitude of
mind typified by the above quotation unques-
tionably accepts competition as the conquer-
ing hero. It is considered that it may be

D

trusted to make its own path smooth. Were this the case *Ethics* would of course not enter into the matter except to give the competitive system free and fair play—"to keep the ring" for it. This accomplished, we might all be content *laisser faire*. To show that the problem is not so simple as is here imagined will be the work of the next chapter.

II.

Our duty in relation to various existing Cir-
cumstances which tend to modify, and in
some cases to nullify, the justice with which
Services to the Community are rewarded
under the Competitive System.

WITHOUT supposing that we are giving a complete enumeration of those circumstances which
disturb the proper operation of the competitive
system, a brief consideration of some of the
most important amongst them will serve our
purpose :—

SOME ARE PARTIALLY REMOV-
ABLE. Under this head we may include :—
(a.) Bad Laws and Bad Customs sanctioned
by Law. For instance, the land laws which
permitted a private ownership in land to grow

up without even making provision for the State's retaining what increased value might accrue independently of improvement of the land itself,—the "unearned increment of value," as it is called.

The laws which similarly failed to reserve to the State the right to the minerals which might be found under the soil.

The laws which have allowed valuable monopoly rights to be enjoyed under State protection without commensurate payment to the State for such privileges, the result being a seeming injustice when it is suggested that the State shall resume the rights without compensation. (Take for instance the question of whether the publicans should be compensated under the Local Taxation Bill of 1890.)

Land laws permitting confiscation of improvements which have been effected by tenants.

Laws providing for primogeniture and entail, and the exorbitant expense of conveying land, all tending to put such land out of the competitive market.

The legalised enclosure of common lands during the 18th and 19th centuries. On this subject Fawcett writes (" Political Economy," Book II., Chapter VIII., pages 237-8) :—
" Since the commencement of the last century
" nearly 5,000,000 acres of land have been
" enclosed. Evidence which has been re-
" peatedly given before Parliamentary Com-
" mittees indisputably proves that in the case
" of almost all these enclosures the interests of
" the poor have been systematically neglected.
" The land which has been thus enclosed has
"sooner or later been added to the large estates
" of neighbouring proprietors. Land over
"which the public could exercise many most
" valuable rights and privileges is, when en-
" closed, converted into private property. The

"opportunities for recreation and enjoyment
"are not only greatly curtailed, but labourers
"who have been accustomed to graze a cow
"or feed poultry upon a common, never again
"have a similar opportunity when the common
"is enclosed.   Those who possess rights of
"common are no doubt, in the first instance,
"compensated ; but the benefits of this com-
"pensation rarely extend beyond those who
"receive it.   The small plot of land which is
"allotted to some commoner is almost certain
"to be sold ; whereas his rights of common
"constituted a property which could not be
"alienated."

We must add to our instances of bad laws
and bad legalised customs, taxation favourable
to the rich.

In most of the cases mentioned above, there
exist appropriate political organisations for
opposing such bad laws and bad legalised

customs as are now remediable, and to these it is open to us to accord support.

Not so evidently to be reckoned amongst the effects of bad laws—though possibly susceptible to influence from legislation, are :—

(b.) Fluctuations in the value of Gold (or whatever is adopted as the standard of value and medium of exchange), which evidently constitute a most serious disturbance to the justice with which services to the community are rewarded. I quote from Professor Herbert S. Foxwell's very interesting monograph, " Irregularity of Employment, and Fluctuations of Prices" (page 45). " Take" . . . "the case of a man who in 1873 borrowed " £142. Prices have since fallen to such an "extent that £92 will now " (Prof. Foxwell writes in 1886) "buy what £142 would have "bought in 1873. Yet the unfortunate debtor

"must pay the full nominal sum borrowed;
"that is to say, his debt is practically increased
"more than 50 per cent." (Prof. Foxwell
attributes some 25 per cent. of this rise *to the
alteration of the value of the standard itself*,
about 25 per cent. to the effect of the credit
cycle, which in 1873 was at its maximum.)
"If, instead of falling, prices had risen in a
"similar degree, the same injustice would have
"resulted. But in this case the creditor would
"have suffered; the debtor would find his debt
"lightened by fifty per cent. Can a system
"which permits of such arbitrary revolutions in
"the distribution of wealth be rational or toler-
"able? I confess it seems to me in the highest
"degree barbarous and uncivilised. The very
"earliest economic writings we have were pro-
"tests against the wrong and mischief caused
"by such changes. Yet nothing has been done.
"The whole fabric of monetary contracts

"is left at the mercy of accident, hanging
"upon the chances of mining discovery."

"What is the apology offered for this singular
"state of things? We are told that it involves
"no injustice, because when people make mone-
"tary contracts they know what they are about.
"If they bargain to receive £5, what they expect
"is about 1¼ ounces of gold, and this Govern-
"ment undertakes to see that they shall receive.
"I venture to assert that this highly theoretical
"view does not represent the common-sense ex-
"pectation of the public. What the ordinary
"man who lends £5 expects, is to receive about
"the same amount of general purchasing power
"as he lent. It is nothing to him how many
"ounces of gold this may at any time happen to
"command" . . . .

"I think, then, there can be no doubt that
"justice and convenience alike would lead us to
"aim at a uniform standard of value. But sup-

" posing such uniformity cannot be attained,
" and that prices must either rise or fall, is there
" anything to choose from a public point of view
" between these two movements ?   It seems to
" me that there is; and that the balance of social
" advantage is in favour of rising prices.   Which-
" ever way prices move, the public are likely in
" one sense to lose.   The middleman is almost
" certain to gain at their expense "   .   .   .   .
" Compared with the dealers, the public are
" always the weaker class, and lose when cus-
" tomary prices are disturbed.   But their loss
" is greatest when prices fall.   When prices
" fall creditors gain at the expense of debtors.
" That is to say, the retired and inactive classes
" gain at the expense of the active and able-
" bodied ; the owners, at the expense of the
" employers, of capital.   Observe, too, that the
" greatest debtor is the public itself, which
" owes the fundholders £740,000,000.   By the

" rise[1] in the value of money since 1873, this
" enormous debt has practically been increased in
" weight twenty-five per cent. The effect is the
" same as if some £180,000,000 of fresh debt
" had been incurred. Wherever fixed payments
" have to be made, the same thing happens."
He goes on to remark: " Suppose that the yard
" measure in common use varied from day to
" day with the temperature, to the great incon-
" venience of trade ; and that some one were to
" propose to ascertain the variation for each day,
" in order that prices might be adjusted to corre-
" spond with it. I think you would say that the
" idea was unnecessarily ingenious. The ob-
" vious remedy would be to compensate the
" measure itself, as you compensate a balance-
" wheel ; or else to choose a measure which did
" not vary at all."

[1] In Prof. Foxwell's pamphlet, "fall" is here misprinted
for "rise." The sentence should read as above.

The importance of the subject of the fluctuation in the value of gold is clearly enough established in Prof. Foxwell's pamphlet; looking at the single department of the monetary reward of labour, we cannot be content that vast changes in the value of money-wages (or as we generally put it, in the value of labour) should "hang on the chances of mining dis-"covery"—that because miners, it may be in South Africa, are more or are less lucky in their finds of gold quartz, our whole industrial system shall be disturbed, and only painfully readjusted after many strikes and their attendant miseries.

But Prof. Foxwell's remedy is not to my mind equally satisfactory. Bimetallism is pointed to as being the most hopeful way of meeting the difficulty; to me it does not appear completely to solve it, though probably it might mitigate the evil. Professor Sidgwick says ("Political Economy," Book III., Chapter IV.

§ 6) a fixed ratio between silver and gold "can
" be permanently maintained—in spite of what
" English monometallists have urged to the
" contrary—if the fluctuations that would other-
" wise take place in the relative market-values
" of the two metals would not be very great in
" proportion to the aggregate of the currency :
" since an increase in the supply of either metal,
" which would tend—if there were no fixed
" ratio—to lower its value, will, under the con-
" ditions of a fixed ratio, tend in the first in-
" stance merely to increase the amount of it
" taken to the mint, and to diminish the mint-
" supply of the other metal ; and so long as the
" increase of supply is not more than enough to
" be absorbed by the readjustment of the mone-
" tary demand, the market-value of the two
" metals will not tend to diverge from the mint
" rate." [On this point, see also Walker's " Political Economy," Part VI., Chap. IX., especi-

ally § 440.]   "On the other hand, it seems
" equally indubitable that when the forces oper-
" ating to raise the value of either metal relatively
" to the other, go beyond a certain point, the
" metal in question will begin to be exported—
" or, if we suppose a rate fixed internationally
" for the whole civilised world, will begin to be
" melted down ; so that the nominally bimetallic
" currency will become substantially a mono-
" metallic currency in the underrated metal"   .
.   .   .   " It is evident that given equal chances
" of fluctuation for both metals " (equal that is
to what they would respectively be under a
monometallic system), "a nominally bimetallic
" currency that from time to time becomes sub-
" stantially monometallic will still be, on the
" whole, more stable than a simply monometallic
" currency."

Whether or not bimetallism is the most complete remedy that can at present be found, we

can at least do what is possible to help inquiry and investigation into the matter.

Questions regarding the *fluctuations in the value of silver*, though less directly affecting us, are in their degree of similar importance.

(c.) Ill-disbursed Charity, which is the direct opposite of ˙a just reward for services rendered to the community, the alms being distributed in proportion to the idleness and plausibility of the beggars. The indirect effect of this twice-cursed " benevolence " is also important, leading as it does to the neglect of duties lettered *b* and *c* in Chapter I., *viz.*, the provision of health and education for those who will otherwise be crippled for the want of them. (See page 43.)

Such ill-disbursed charity is almost universally acknowledged to be an evil. How are we to avoid it? It is plain we must not give to all comers and all askers, but if we consistently

refuse to all, though it is true that we shall in
the long run be doing a great deal less mischief, we shall encourage in ourselves a hard-
hearted and indifferent attitude of mind to
many of the sorrows of the world. Yet not
one man in a hundred has time properly to
investigate for himself the genuineness of the
appeals that are brought before him, and to
ascertain all the complicated bearings of such
cases. On the whole then it appears to be a
proper matter for corporate action. By the
co-operation of numbers of people, and by
recognising that officers must be specially retained and paid to devote their whole time to investigation, much can be done. A good Charity
Organisation Society should be considered
one of the primary and most essential institu-
tions of every town. It by no means follows,
however, because *investigation* cannot generally
be properly done except by delegating the

work to a society, that the work of *caring for* the very poor—real " charity "—should be so delegated. · A Charity Organisation Society should help people to be charitable ; it is never intended that it should take from them the obligation.

OTHERS OF THE MODIFYING CAUSES REQUIRE REFORM RATHER THAN REMOVAL.

(d.) The Poor Law, and the Bankruptcy System, both avowedly aiming at a removal of the penalties which would be suffered under the present system in cases where individuals have been quite without worldly success. A consideration which has no doubt led to the recognition, side by side with the competitive system, of these other systems which, within their own spheres of influence, so completely nullify the justice of its operations, is that justice must be

E

tempered with mercy. We may question indeed whether justice itself demands the extreme logical penalties of the competitive
system in a state of things where, as we are
beginning to realise, the competitive system is
by no means the only important influence at
work in determining men's material success in
life. There would be much more to be said
for the abolition of the poor law and the bankruptcy system, were no important economic in-
fluences extant independent of, and in some
cases opposed to, competition.

There is little doubt that the Poor Law is
susceptible of improvement and reform. The
Rev. H. V. Mills's " Poverty and the State "
is an interesting essay in this direction, and
something like the line of reform he advocates
has the support of Mr. Charles Booth (editor
and part author of " Labour and Life of the
People" in London). The author's suggestion

is, that we shall do away with poor houses, and substitute for them settlements in the home country, the colonists in which shall, in part by agricultural labour on the land attached to each home-colony, in part by industrial work, all under State supervision and control, support themselves. This Mr. Mills believes they would soon be able to do without being any longer a burden on the rest of the community. The scheme as being educative instead of demoralising invites attention on grounds other than the direct economic advantage claimed for it. A very similar proposal is one of the chief features of General William Booth's scheme of Social Reform, formulated in " In Darkest England and the Way Out."

The reform of the bankruptcy system seems to be especially needed in relation to dishonest speculation. It is difficult to see why a man who plunges into a hazardous venture, knowing that if he wins he will gain a fortune, whereas if he loses he will not be able to supply one, should not be imprisoned as much as any other thief or fraudulent person.

(*e.*) *Monopolies* are from the nature of the case inconsistent with competition. The right to monopolise is sometimes conferred or assumed by Government; sometimes it is sought by combination amongst individuals, but success by this means is not generally long retained. A case however of the successful and continued lowering of wage below the "normal" or "fair" level by means of combination, seems to be found in the agreements amongst farmers in some agricultural districts respecting the remuneration of their labourers :—

"The farmers are few in number, most of "them have known one another from childhood, "and there is generally a tacit understanding

"among them as to the rate at which they are
"to pay their labourers. If any of them were
"to break through the understanding, parti-
"cularly if he were to do it with the object of
"drawing men away from another farmer, he
"would suffer in the esteem of those for whose
"opinion he cares most. In fact, 'there is
"'rarely much competition for labour on the
"'part of employers *within* a trade in a parti-
"'cular place, unless there be competition for it
"'from *without*' (Cliffe Leslie. "Land System,'
"p. 371). And unless there is a manufacturing
"industry in the neighbourhood, competition
"from without seldom makes its appearance in
"an agricultural village."

"On the other hand, labourers are in the
"position of sellers of perishable commodities :
"in some cases they may like to rest from work
"for a while, and have a play-day ; but if they
"are kept long from work and wages, they all,

"and particularly the married men, suffer much
"from losing the price of part of their labour.
"Agricultural labourers seldom think of seeking
"work outside the parish in which they were
"born ; and thus are sometimes at the mercy
"of a few farmers who may perhaps decide at
"a market dinner what wages to allow."
("Economics of Industry," by Alfred Marshall,
and Mary Paley Marshall, pp. 184-5.)   Similar
conditions probably exist to a less extent in other
employments which are unprotected by Unions
and where the range of economic intelligence is
not high.

"Rings" are not generally of a very permanent character, neither do I think that it has
been proved that Trade-Unions in England
have at their disposal a monopoly of different
varieties of labour, but it is no doubt a result
that might conceivably be attained.   Where
there were not found to be stronger counter-con-

siderations, it might possibly be well to counteract by legislation, combinations that had been
proved to amount to monopoly.[1]   The multipli-
cation of "Trusts" and their growing importance
is engaging the attention of the Legislature in
the United States.

(f.) Custom, even in this country, sometimes
overrides competition, though to a very small
extent when compared with countries in a state
of less commercial advancement,—India for
example.   The fees of professional men are
for instance to some extent regulated in this
way.   If however we contrast the position of
a celebrated Q.C., or a specialist much sought
after, with that of a young man beginning to
practise either at the bar or in medicine, we
shall see that though custom regulates pro-

---

[1] For a treatment of this subject, the reader is referred to
Prof. Marshall's " Principles of Economics," Book V.,
Chapter viii., and also to § 5 of Chapter ix.

fessional fees, competition has something to say as to professional salaries. Custom still has an important though a diminishing influence in determining the remuneration of certain branches of labour, especially in domestic service. The theory of non-competing groups of industry (see pages 28 to 36) exhibits custom as an important element in hindering free competition amongst labour. (It is however by no means the only element; lack of information, of intelligence, of capital, etc., also have to be counted with.) Each custom has to be considered on its own merits; many (*e.g.*, that which regulates doctors' fees) will be found to tend to mitigate those extreme variations in the distribution of wealth, for which other circumstances disturbing the results of competition are in large part responsible. It will not in these cases be found that the first step to be taken in purifying our present system is to combat such customs.

The case is sometimes far otherwise however; for instance, as far as we regard the non-competition of different groups of labour as due to custom, it should doubtless be fought against.

Commercial Immorality requires not Reform but COMPLETE REMOVAL; but this can only follow an ALTERATION of ETHICAL STANDARDS.

(*g.*) We remarked in Chapter I. the necessity (in order to give the competitive system free scope in its action) of there being some efficient means for the suppression of crime. To obviate injustice in the reward of services to the community, it is further necessary that *dishonesty which is not actually criminal* shall be done away with.

By far the most important phase of dishonesty which we have to consider in this connection is Commercial Immorality. The four principal forms it assumes are :—

Bad work and adulteration.

Immoral and useless trades.

Bribery.

Deception.

The obligation to do away with such dishonesty cannot yet be said to be generally recognised, but it is surely imperative.   For my own part I place chivalrous personal honesty in the forefront of the ethical duties in relation to wealth, for the double reason that ideal honesty, being rarely found, is, perhaps more than any other of our moral ideals, in want of reinforcement by example; and because I think self-imposed and absolutely rigid honesty would do more than any other one thing, to prevent the accumulation in few hands of large masses of wealth illegitimately gained.

I am aware that amongst commercial men there exist certain codes of honour; some maintain a high standard of uprightness, whilst some permit alarming laxity. On certain elementary points however they are in substantial agreement. It would for example be generally recognised, that one merchant left by himself in the office of another would not act honourably in reading letters or telegrams that might be lying on the table. Yet in one aspect such a feeling may be considered conventional, and would be inadmissible if the competitive system were interpreted to warrant the acquisition of advantage to oneself *by every means in one's power.* But if it is possible that by mutual consent *some* such limitations should exist, it makes one hopeful of the feasability of establishing at some future time a code in conformity with the strictest ideas of honesty and honour in other spheres of life. In such a code such articles as the following would find a natural place :—

Bad Work (such as building houses of bad

materials, laying drains badly and the like), and *Adulteration* (weighting silk with clay, mixing water with milk, etc.), should be considered dishonourable, and by a slight extension of the principle, any efforts directed merely to making articles more saleable, without at the same time making them more useful to the purchaser, should be disapproved.

It should be considered dishonourable to obtain money from, or be engaged in, a trade that the individual considers *immoral.* In extreme instances this principle receives some recognition; to receive an enhanced rent from a house of ill fame would be condemned by a very large part of the community; many of those amongst the teetotalers who think consuming alcoholic drink in itself an immoral action, would have nothing to do with brewing businesses. This principle might I think with advantage be carried out much more strictly and a great deal further ; and if it were so, we should be led to the same conclusion that we arrived at above when we were considering the effects of bad work. Besides asking the question as to whether any work or commercial enterprise is profitable to himself, every individual is bound to inquire whether it is likely to be really of service to the community. If this were recognised it would be dishonourable not only to do immoral, but to do useless, business.

Commercial Bribery (under its various names of " palm-oil," "sweetening," "commissions," and the like) should be considered dishonourable. The characteristic of a commercial bribe is, that a man nominally in the service of one employer is also paid by another without the knowledge of the first. The fact is kept secret from the legitimate employer, because his interests (which the man is paid to forward) will in some way suffer. If we pay another man's servant directly or indirectly, keeping the fact secret from the employer, we may feel sure that we are trying to make the man neglect the duty that he has engaged to perform, and for which he will be paid, and that we are bribing. It is still true that "ye cannot serve two masters." Taking such bribes is of course as dishonourable as giving them; sometimes, where the bribed person is in a powerful position, it is much more so.

Deception in business should be considered dishonourable. There are of course legitimate *secrets* in business, but where facts are professed to be disclosed, they should be disclosed truthfully. To illustrate my meaning I will consider the different positions of a wholesale and of a retail trader in fixing the prices of his goods. The wholesale trader may legitimately get the highest price he can for his goods by the "higgling of the market." He is dealing with those who are as well versed as he is in the conditions of his trade. The lowest price he is prepared to take is his secret, and broadly speaking he is justified in getting as much more as he can from any individual with whom he is dealing, so long as he is perfectly candid about the character of his goods, and makes no effort to deceive the buyer about any of the conditions of the market, etc. The retail dealer on the other hand is doing business with those out of the trade; the supposition is that he fixes upon the lowest price he considers he can afford to take, and tells the public what it is. For *him* therefore *it is not honest to have more than one price*, although it may be perfectly legitimate for the wholesale trader to sell at one price to one man, and at another to another.

I have not considered it necessary to give examples of the various forms taken by trade

immorality. Those who have not had personal
experience of many of them will find the subject treated in some detail in Mr. Herbert
Spencer's well-known essay on " The Morals
of Trade."

The object that almost every business man
now sets before himself, so far as his business
dealings are concerned (though not necessarily
or generally in the other relations of life), is at
all hazards to secure his own interests. But another ambition at which he might aim, is to be not
only scrupulously, but *chivalrously* honest in all
his dealings ; to be really and not merely pro-
fessedly anxious that he himself should suffer
rather than that any interests which he had
undertaken should not be cared for; to deem the
taking of a petty advantage of another because
his actions were not being closely watched, as
much out of the question as he would the taking of money from the till of a shopman whose

back happened to be turned. What a new feature the introduction of such principles would bring into commercial life! I suppose nothing can be much more unpoetical than the ordinary routine of an office. Assuming a case where all are faithful servants to the firm, each is bent on obtaining advantages here and there for the company which employs him. If in place of this each were intent with the full consent, and indeed at the instigation of the heads of the firm, on dealing out justice coupled with open-handed generosity, an element of strong interest, of romance almost, would pervade the whole system. The idea of poetry's centring in a ledger seems incongruous enough, but if the record of figures told of determination to carry out engagements faithfully, cost what it might; if it told of heavy disbursements in consequence of refusal to acquiesce, or take any part, in the prevalent corruptions and abuses of the day; if

F

it told of unbending resistance to oppression,
and never-tiring determination to hunt down
dishonesty; if it told of a desire to do good
work for a moderate remuneration;—the idea
might not be very far from realisation. Let
business men ask themselves if their offices
would not then have a charm which they had
not before. Many of them devote a mere
fraction of their lives to the enjoyment of the
wealth which all the rest of their existence is
spent in accumulating ; and many feel that the
major portion of life is only worth living for
the sake of this residuum of time. But why
should not the life of the office, as well as home
life, be worthy ?

Meanwhile the bearing on the question of
the condition of the poor, both directly and
indirectly, would be very important. For example manufactured things would be *good ;*
they would not be made to sell but to fulfil

their nominal function, and we should hear no more of bad material in houses, or of adulterated food and drink.

Prospective as well as retrospective considerations complicate our view of what our attitude should be towards

(*h.*) *Hereditary Wealth*, which, besides being awarded irrespectively of the services rendered to the community by the individual who receives it, may perpetuate the results of all the above seven other disturbing causes, and those also of crime, and of the infirmity and ignorance of others. For its abolition we are probably not yet ripe ; the unit amongst us for wealth-distribution is to a great extent the family rather than the individual, and few amongst us are prepared to leave our children without such special provision as we can contrive ; but it is a question whether something may not be done

in the direction of increasing by gradual steps
the already considerable taxes payable on inherited personal property by an extension of
the principle of the estate duty of 1889, which
imposes an additional *ad valorem* tax of one
per cent. on all estates amounting in value to
£10,000 and upwards; and whether real property cannot advantageously be put upon the
same footing as personal property by making
it liable to probate duty, and by making
succession duty payable (like legacy duty) on full
capital value, instead of on the value of the life-
interest of the inheritor, and in other minor
points. (See "A Handbook to the Death
Duties," by S. Buxton, M.P., and G. S. Barnes.
1890. Murray.)

When we take into account the full force of
the circumstances above enumerated, of bad
Laws; Ill-disbursed Charity; a Fluctuating
Standard of Value; the Bankruptcy System,

and the Poor Law; Monopoly; Custom; and Commercial Immorality ; all handed on from generation to generation by a system of hereditary transmission of wealth ; when we further consider that of these eight disturbing causes some can at present only be removed in part, others not at all, we shall surely be willing to acknowledge that because a man does not flourish under the present system, it does not *necessarily* follow that he is either a knave or a fool.

III.

Socialism.

IN the first chapter, whilst justifying the doctrine of the old " Manchester School," that the competitive system tended to bring about certain desirable results, we saw reason to discard their conclusions in favour of ' laissez faire,"[1] there being necessity for much ethical action in aiding the completion of those processes that (under the automatic action of the

[1] In a foot-note in his "Principles of Economics " (Vol. I., page 54), Professor Marshall says: "Their favourite phrase " (*i.e.*, that of the Physiocrats), " *laissez faire, laissez aller,* is "commonly misapplied now. *Laissez faire* means that "anyone should be allowed to make what things he likes, "and as he likes; that all trades should be open to every-"body; that Government should not, as the Colbertists "insisted, prescribe to manufacturers the fashion of their "cloth." In the text I use the term *laissez faire* in that other sense in which it is now generally understood.

competitive system) are so slow as to cause much suffering by the way, and in improving the environment so that the conditions for competition may be as perfect as possible,—a necessary antecedent to its action's being beneficent. The human frame is capable of good work, but that is no justification for our giving it no medicine when it is ill, or of our failing to provide it with fresh air, food, and drink at all times.

In the second chapter we examined a number of economic forces existing side by side with, but in themselves independent of, the competitive system. We found that in relation to these also we had ethical duties, and we considered what they were.

Many of the evils resulting (1) from the clogging and hampering of a purely competitive system, and (2) from the economic forces which are independent of the competitive system, are not likely to be immediately removed or reformed, perhaps they never can be, and it will be the task of another chapter to consider what courses of action are desirable as tending to do away with their ill effects.

That the courses indicated by the considerations we have already reviewed are full of difficulty, and that more serious difficulties still face us in the considerations yet to come, is clear, and we shall not do right if we neglect to investigate a reputed short-cut to the more equitable distribution of wealth.

SOCIALISM says in effect that the rewards for social services rendered under the competitive system are so far from being just in virtue of its supposed automatic adjustments, and are so much disturbed by the modifying causes enumerated in Chapter II., as entirely to destroy the usefulness of that system and to make it desirable that it should be abolished.

Definitions —

COMMUNISM aims at an equalisation of material wealth.

SOCIALISM seeks to reward services to the community, not proportionately to their value as estimated by the public opinion of the community, but proportionately to the endeavour made in rendering them (also estimated by the public opinion of the community, but in a different way).

The estimation according to public opinion of the value of services to individuals is automatically recorded by the competitive system. There is no such automatic assessment of the value of effort in the service of the whole community; such valuation has therefore to be made on a more or less arbitrary basis.

The ideas which are essentially characteristic of Communism and Socialism are I believe expressed in the above definitions, though the derivations

of the two words have frequently led to the attach-
ment to them of more stringent significations.

Thus Communism is sometimes said to aim
at the enjoyment of all things *in common ;* but
in the case of a great many things it is impossible that there should be *common* use ; one
particular slice of bread must go into one
particular mouth; one particular shirt must
clothe one particular back; and though common
public meals, common pasture lands, and so
forth, may be the most practicable way of
securing an equal division of the advantages of
property, it is I believe the equality of advantage itself, not the community of its enjoyment,
that is the root ideal of the imagined system.

The word Socialism evidently points to social,
or corporate action, and this is often taken to
mean more than the assessment and control by
the community of the distribution of wealth, and
defined as the actual organisation of industry by

the State. Thus Lord Salisbury, speaking in the House of Lords, May 19th, 1890, said :—
" I take Socialism in its strict meaning to be,
" for the State to do a thing which hitherto and
" usually has been done by private people for the
" sake of gain. I believe that that is often a
" very unwise thing. But sometimes it is a
" very wise thing. There is nothing so social-
" istic as the Mint or the Post Office."

Now no doubt the meaning here assigned to Socialism must be accepted as a rough and ready expression of a popular idea, such as would be suited to the purposes of debate, rather than as an attempt at a scientific defini-tion (were it otherwise it would be pertinent to point out that the Mint and the Post Office have not hitherto and usually been undertaken by private people for the sake of gain) ; Lord Salisbury merely wishes to indicate that the essential characteristic of Socialism is State

organisation of industry.   Now State organisation of industry implies that the community
through its representatives undertakes certain
work to the exclusion of certain individuals.
If the work were done by private individuals
certain profits would accrue which would go into their pockets.   If the State make similar
profits, such profits go to the diminution of
taxation ; if it make no profits, the services are
rendered to the public more cheaply than they
otherwise would be.   In either case there is a
slight admixture of Communism.   Wealth that
might otherwise be appropriated by individuals
goes to the benefit of the whole community.
But it is of Communism *not* of Socialism[1] as I
have defined it that there is a touch, and it is
important to observe that it is *only* a touch.   To
speak of such an institution as the Post Office

[1] It is true however that to a certain small extent
Socialism is included in Communism.   On this point see
pages 123-4.

as communistic is very like the notion (which by the way I am informed is *not* good law), that an action can be brought against a man for "false imprisonment" because he shuts you out of one particular field, the idea being that in the legal sense you are "imprisoned," although you have for your prison-house all the world except that particular field.

The Post Office of course is managed by the State, not because of the advantages of Communism, but for quite other reasons. The Communism involved may in fact be regarded as a slight counteracting inconvenience; and were all industries managed by the State, the inconvenience might be considerable : we might, indeed, be more in the position of a village hemmed in on every side by closed fields ; if a play on words may be pardoned, our "false" might become *true* imprisonment.

Lord Salisbury's definition, whilst including

the Mint as essentially socialistic, would not cover an Eight Hours' Bill. I on the other hand think that the Mint is not socialistic, but that an Eight Hours' Bill is. If indeed the officers of the Mint and the Post Office were paid what is called a "fair wage," and their services were not obtained (as in the case of private firms) at the lowest market-price—then, in that respect, I should say they were socialistic ; but it would appear that the Post Office is in this particular more uncompromisingly unsocialistic than are many private firms.

Having so far endeavoured to clear our ideas as to what meaning we should attach to the word Socialism, I must avow that I cannot view hopefully the proposal that the competitive shall abdicate in favour of a socialistic system.

The *primâ facie* case for the overthrow of competition seems to me to be weak ; for the evils complained of appear to spring not from anything inherent in the system itself, but rather from excrescences on, or hindrances to, its growth, or from causes entirely independent of it, and in some cases opposed to it.

But not only do I think the *primâ facie* case for the proposed remedy weak, the remedy itself appears to me inadmissible. Out of the many arguments against Socialism, I shall confine myself mainly to two ; the first, though not applicable in an ideal state of morality, is so strongly operative *now* that it would be madness to ignore it,—it is that the competitive system *at present* furnishes the most powerful available incentive to the due fulfilment of services to the community. The second as far as I can see always must be cogent, for I conceive that the competitive system *always will be* the only test of whether given work is required by the community or not.

I. The general experience is that in spite of the

circumstances which do so much to modify
its power, the competitive system at present
furnishes in the majority of cases the most
powerful available incentive to the due fulfilment of services to the community.

Consider for example co-operation, which
means an arrangement allowing the individual
workers to share in the results of an enterprise
launched amidst the competitive system. Increased energy and effectiveness follow. From
one point of view it is true co-operation is opposed to competition. *Wi'hin a given group*
those who would be able to secure the greatest
:dvantage in a state of free competition, agree
to share some of this advantage with others ;
but this is only in order that their competition
as a group may be more effective, and further,
it is in the belief that *every individual in the
group will in the long run profit from a material
point of view.* Just because some restraint is

put on the inner competition, the outer competition is felt directly in a way that it pre-
viously was not, and the strength of the competitive impulse as a whole on the individual,
is rendered more forcible. We shall see in a
moment that this is so, if we reflect that co-operation is advocated not on the grounds that the
appeal to the self-interest of the individual is
lessened, but that it is strengthened.

It is admitted that schemes of " profit-sharing," initiated by employers, have the greatest
chance of permanent acceptance when they are
profitable to themselves as well as to the employed. Schemes of this sort, however beneficial from a philanthropic point of view, if they
do not give some promise of immediate or
remote advantage, or at least recoupment to,
the employers, are distinctly less likely to be
launched generally than if they can be shown
to be likely to be profitable to them. I am not

saying that this ought to be so ; I am only adducing it as an instance of the power of the acquisition of material advantage for the individual, as an impetus to work; and the competitive system is the one that allows each one to seek his own material advantage in the way he considers most effective. If even the class of *entrepreneurs*, powerful as they are, and for the most part rich, open to many of the wider considerations of the social state, and susceptible to charitable appeals, if even this class is as a rule unwilling to work except for personal (as opposed to collective) gain, what can we as yet hope from the general mass of struggling units ?

Is it not indeed very questionable whether, in spite of the apparent wide-spread adoption of socialistic views, there are in England more than a mere handful of sincere Socialists, that is to say of persons who sincerely, and if necessary

practically, prefer the social to their individual
gain?   I make no question of the genuineness of
the professions of many of the leaders, nor of
the good faith even of the rank and file ; but
of the latter an overwhelming majority have
never been in a position to put their socialistic
principles to a practical test.   The modifica-
tions of property-ownership which they demand
would (as it seems to them) almost invariably
have the effect of bettering their material position individually as well as collectively.   They
are in fact played upon by precisely the same
motives as the members of a trade-ring, or men
on strike for higher pay.   How can we be sure,
how can their leaders be sure, how even can
they themselves be sure, that it is the socialistic
and not the individualistic motive that exercises
so powerful a sway ?   Without wishing to treat
the socialistic professions ungenerously, I cannot grant it as being satisfactorily proved that

even all those who profess Socialism are in
reality prepared to forego individual advantage
where it clashes with the prosperity of the
community, because generally speaking it is
with them as it is with the co-operators, they
believe that every individual Socialist amongst
them will in the long run profit from a material
point of view.   To give some authority for this
view, I quote from the "Fabian Essays in
Socialism" (published by the Fabian Society,
1889), which is I suppose the nearest approach
to an official declaration of the views of
educated English Socialists that we have.   In
the last essay, entitled "The Outlook," the
writer, Mr. Hubert Bland, says (page 204) :

"The coming struggle between 'haves' and
"'have nots' will be a conflict of parties each
"perfectly conscious of what it is fighting about
"and fully alive to the life and death importance
"of the issues at stake" . . . "it is to the

"suffering—the hunger, the despair of to-
" morrow's dinner, the anxiety about the next
" new pair of trousers,—wrought by the increas-
" ing economic pressure upon the enfranchised
" and educated proletariat, that we must look to
" awaken that free self-consciousness which will
" give the economic changes political expression,
" and enable the worker to make practical use of
" the political weapons which are his." Could
anything be more frank ? To those of us who
are not members of the Fabian Society they
do not appear to be new ideas at all, but the
distressingly familiar principles of greed and
grab.

I cannot resist quoting further (p. 211) Mr.
Bland's description of the " desperately silly "
abnegation of the radicals, who are open to
other considerations than personal advantage
in political matters. " The young artizan on
" five-and-twenty shillings a week, who with his

" wife and children occupies two rooms in a
" ' model,' and who is about as likely to become
"a Lama as a leaseholder, will shout himself
"hoarse over Leasehold's Enfranchisement, and
"sweat great drops of indignation at the
"plunder of rich West End tradesmen by
"rich West End landlords. The 'out of work'
"whose last shirt is in pawn, will risk his skull's
"integrity in Trafalgar Square in defence of
"Mr. O'Brien's claim to dress in gaol like a
"gentleman."

It is almost a pity that at this point Mr.
Bland seems to become dimly conscious that he
is advocating a lower and not a higher standard
of morality, and that he spoils the effect of his
sarcasm by adding : " Of course, all this is very
"touching : indeed, to be quite serious, it
"indicates a nobility of character and breadth of
"human sympathy in which lies our hope of
"social salvation."

Now, looking at the overcrowded condition of certain industries, women workers in match factories for instance, or men workers on tramways, does not the hardness of the conditions of their lives constitute an impetus (though evidently a very insufficient impetus to many of them) to abandon doing that work for which there are already so sadly too many volunteers, and to undertake other work which the community cannot find enough people to do ? If· this impetus were removed, would not one result be that fewer would go to be domestic servants and farm labourers in the colonies (where they are wanted), and more remain idle and starving, hoping for the reversion of the place of the comfortably-paid girl in the match factory, or conductor on the tramway ?

If it is answered, " *No*, because these poor " people are so beaten down by mental and " physical starvation that they have neither

"energy nor intelligence to do the best for
"themselves that might be done,"[1] the objection
is insufficient, for the rejoinder is found in the
fulfilment of the duties now generally recognised by society and enumerated in Chapter I.,
which will have to be supplemented by the
ethical duties pointed to in Chapters II. and
IV. People must not be allowed to be
crippled for want either of the bodily or mental

[1] "If we consider the population of the more squalid
"sections of any city, we can only conclude that contrary to
"the assumption of the economist, the more miserable men
"are, the less and not the more likely they are to seek and
"find a better place in society and industry. Their
"poverty, their ignorance, their superstitious fears and,
"perhaps more than all, the apathy that comes with a
"broken spirit, bind them in their place and to their fate.
"To apply to human beings in their condition maxims de-
"rived from the contemplation of the 'economic man,' is
"little less than preposterous. Such populations do not
"migrate, they abide in their lot, sinking lower in helpless-
"ness, hopelessness, and squalor; economic forces have
"not the slightest virtue either to give them higher wages,
"or to make them deserving of higher wages." Professor
Francis A. Walker, "The Wages Question," page 188.

equipment necessary to work in harmony with the competitive system.

If it is objected that the juster way for the community to act would be to employ exactly so many workers as its requirements might dictate, to pay them the average reward for the labour and skill expended, and leave the rest without employment in that industry, so that they would be *compelled* to seek other avocations,—the first point which arises in reply is that it is difficult to define the requirements of the community, that for many things they are practically in inverse proportion to the price. But if it is further urged that the requirements of the community might be defined to be such as would fix the effective demand at the point where the labour employed received a reward equal to that paid on the average in other departments of labour for an equal amount of effort or skill, (*i.e.*, what economists have called the " natural " or " normal wage "), we have an intelligible demand made upon us, but one that it would be immensely difficult to carry out, and one that we shall find on examination is likely to bring about results the opposite of those which we seek. It would seem almost impossible accurately to assess the comparative intensity of various kinds of work and skill.[1] Nevertheless it is without doubt true that one can put one's finger on instances where it may be said with certainty that the amount of work and skill expended is less highly rewarded than

[1] By equal intensity of work and skill is here meant work and skill which, *if they were equally well directed*, would be equally serviceable to the community, putting aside for the moment the question of whether they actually *are* directed equally well. If a garden requires to be tended by one gardener and three men employ themselves in it, the work and skill of the three men are accounted three times as intense as that of one of them. The work and skill of an eccentric who takes coal to Newcastle are as intense as those of him who pursues the beaten path of commerce in shipping it from that port.

the same amount of work and skill in other departments of labour. One may take the London needle-woman as an example. How comes it about that this state of things does not right itself by the supposed automatic action of the competitive system? That on the other hand it continues through generations?

The explanation is no doubt to a large extent found in the non-competition (dwelt upon in Chapter I.) of various groups of industry. With this all-important fact in our minds, let us consider the ways that may be proposed of treating the problem of a group of labourers in which there are far too many individuals, who are in consequence paid a miserable wage. We take for example our London seamstresses. Shall we pay them all round a " fair wage ?"— *i.e.*, a wage equal to that paid in other industries for an equal amount of labour and skill? If we do so we remove the danger-signals which

actually prevent many workers from entering
the overcrowded avocation, and we take away
the inducements to mobility of labour, which to
a very large extent cause a fair distribution
of labour between industries in the same competing group, and even cause some few of the
exceptional workers to find their employment in
groups of industry which are generally speaking non-competing. The causes which have
already been enough to make the industry overcrowded are intensified and perpetuated.

Shall we then employ only as many women
as there is an effective demand for at a "fair
"wage?" If we do so, what is to become of
the rest? A few more perhaps than might
otherwise have been the case will, through the
very compulsion of the situation, make their
way into other ordinarily non-competing groups
of industry ; but most of those who are refused
employment will not; and instead of being left

with a frightfully inadequate wage, they will be left with nothing.

Possibly it may be said that there is not much to choose between the two. But it would be immensely difficult to determine by a dogmatic selection from without, who were to be admitted and who were to be refused admission to a given industry. At present *all* the workers in an industry which becomes over-crowded feel the pressure of the automatic penalty alike, and as the evil grows the pressure grows also. *Some* of those who would otherwise enter or remain in the industry do not do so. There is a tendency that these shall be in the first place those who are least able, in proportion to their other qualifications, to perform the particular work demanded in the industry. The competitive system then tends to select for expulsion from the industry those who are least economically employed in it.

This might conceivably be done by a process of selection under a socialistic system; but we have further to consider a most essential feature in the case, *viz.*, that those whom it is least desirable to retain in a given industry are of two sorts—those who are too good for the industry, and those who are. not good enough. The former class, those who might advantageously be put to a superior class of work, are those whom the competitive system tempts upwards; the latter class, the dregs of that particular grade of labour, are those who would be squeezed downwards by the proposed method.   But it is the lower, not the higher end of the industrial scale that is overcrowded, so that we could not view with satisfaction the substitution for a system which does something to tempt upwards from the overcrowded industries into the less crowded ones, one that would (by making their present position more secure and comfortable) diminish the inducement to those capable of better work, to ascend, and instead ˙ force downwards into still more crowded grades below, those who are least fit and able.

But it is argued by the idealists that anxiety for the general welfare should be, and will be, as powerful an impetus to usefulness of living as is individual gain.

That it should be I am not only willing to admit, but anxious to urge,—that at some future time it will be, I almost dare to hope,—but that it *is* (within any large circle of acceptance) cannot surely be maintained. Throughout the world of commerce and of trade the opposite doctrine is everywhere uppermost in men's minds. True, more and more willingness is shown to join large combinations, but the good sought is that of the combination, not of the community. I have shown reason for thinking that this is true even of the combination of Socialists.

" But," it may further be urged, " it does not " follow that because preference of the general " weal to self is not as yet a largely accepted " doctrine, that individuals who *do* accept it " should not act on altruistic principles." Certainly it does not follow. But acting on this line is a very different thing to taking for granted in defiance of all evidence that great masses of people are prepared to act in accordance with the self-abnegatory principle. Yet this is emphatically what the socialist pro- posals assume. Quoting again from Mr. Hubert Bland, we find it stated on page 212 that — " Socialism is the common holding " of the means of production and exchange, " and *the holding of them for the equal benefit* " *of all.*" Now the common holding of the means of production and exchange means that

the *entrepreneur* class would not be tempted by
the present high rewards that attend their
successful undertakings, to put forth their full
abilities. But the importance of the *entrepreneur* class is immense. Prof. Walker says
("Wages Question," pp. 252-3): "These men
"constitute a class strictly limited in numbers,
"and dealing most despotically, as indeed they
"must, with the outside world. The conditions
"of admission are a long self-initiation, a high
"premium of immediate loss, and a great
"degree of uncertainty as to ultimate success."
. . . . "M. Courcelle-Seneuil, in his *Opera-
"tions de Banque*, has grouped the qualities the
"employer should possess: 'du jugement, du
"'bon sens, de la fermeté, de la décision, une
"'appréciation froide et calme, une intelligence
"'ouverte et vigilante, peu d'imagination, beau-
"'coup de mémoire et d'application.'"
Unless it is disputed that individual gain —

individual greed if you will—*is* at present
the paramount impulse which induces them
to work, we can only conclude that they,
the organisers of industry, will succeed in
evading the efforts of the State to curtail their
reward, or that the community will no longer
enjoy the results of their invaluable labours,
and as Walker says (page 250), "Nothing costs
"the working-classes so dearly in the long run
"as the bad or merely common-place conduct
"of business." Similarly if the means of production and exchange are held for the equal
benefit of all, which means I suppose that all
are to be paid the same wages for equally
arduous work, whether it is wanted by the community or not, until the social welfare is
held more dear, the individual worker able
and otherwise willing to do more valuable
work for the community than others, will
either evade the regulations by which it is

sought to pay him no more highly than the rest
or through mere sloth and apathy slip back into
doing work which is comparatively valueless.
Even therefore if Socialism is a practicable
system AFTER the moral revolution which shall
make each man prefer the good of the community to his own, it is *essential* that measures
that assume the acceptance of the principle of
self-sacrifice by both *entrepreneurs* and workmen shall be preceded by their conversion to it.

The new impulse must be supplied before
you may dare to remove the old one. An
alteration of our arrangements on this basis,
if it is not to be disastrous, must be preceded
by a *moral* revolution.

To those who are already prepared to practise
self-abnegation in regard to wealth, there is
most abundant scope for action without their
taking a course which assumes against all the
evidence the general acceptance of the prin-

ciple. I have tried to show that this latter course would be attended by disastrous results, and surely this is not to be wondered at when it rests on an assumption that we all know to be a lie.

But if it is true that socialistic legislation introduced into a competitive community must be disastrous, how comes it about that much legislation which is accounted socialistic has already been adopted in England and with admittedly beneficial results ? We have a Poor Law for instance, we have Factory Laws, we have a State-managed Post Office.

Considering the number and importance of the excrescences on our competitive system enumerated in Chap. II., it is quite conceivable that evils should have grown up in our system of trade that have nothing whatever to do with competition, which it is necessary to try and remove. In removing great evils that have arisen in this way, the competitive system may be incidentally trenched upon, and to the extent that it is hampered the legislation may be an evil, and yet the good that it does in other directions may be considerably more than a counterpoise to the evil.

An examination of the Poor Law from this point of view is very instructive. The *à priori* case for a Poor Law is that it is possible that men may, through no fault of their own, be reduced to the greatest poverty. They may have been thrown out of work by the invention of a new mechanical process or a change of fashion which has rendered their particular aptitude no longer in demand. They may have met with accidents, or their health may have failed them. They may have been ruined by bad laws, or indirectly by the fluctuation in the value of gold, or they may have been unable to cope with commercial immorality practised at their expense. A good case is

here made out for legislation for the poor,
quite independently of any ill effects of the
competitive system.

But relief given without discrimination may
not only benefit those who have failed *in spite*
of the tendency of the competitive system to
reward ability and industry, but also those who
have failed *because* of the tendency of the competitive system to discourage inability and
idleness.   If the counteraction to the latter
becomes a much more important feature than
the alleviation of the former, the law is certainly directly opposed to the competitive
system ; it is a true instance of a socialistic
law introduced amongst a competitive community.   This was the state of our Poor Law
during the first third of the century.   Fawcett
says (Fifth Ed., page 578) :—

" Allowance in aid of wages and recklessness
" in granting outdoor relief were gradually

" pauperising the country, and the rates, which
"were constantly increasing, absorbed a large
"portion of the profits of industry." In 1834
the new Poor Law was passed. Men were no
longer encouraged recklessly to shirk the demands made upon them by the competitive
system ; on the contrary they were discouraged
from doing so, and vigorous restrictions were
imposed upon able-bodied paupers. " The allow-
"ance system, with its manifold abuses, which
"was now abolished, had directly encouraged
"voluntary pauperism. The workhouse test
"provided a most salutary check, and the
"greatest possible good would have resulted if it
"had been made obligatory upon local authorities
"to apply this test to all able-bodied paupers."
(Fawcett, Seventh Edition, p. 593.)

The encouragement to idleness was thus in
a great part removed. The failure to encourage
ability has not been so successfully met, and

the proposals of Mills and Booth on this point are worthy of consideration. (See pages 66-67.)

Again, the importance of the success of the Factory Acts lies, not in their opposition to the competitive system, but in their opposition to things that either have nothing to do with the competitive system one way or the other, or that themselves go to undermine the effects of that system. A great part of the Factory Acts are akin to the legislation aimed towards the prevention of cruelty to children and cruelty to animals. They protect powerless young children and women who are comparatively powerless. Other regulations endeavour to secure sanitation.

Now it is doubtful whether these humanitarian regulations really make it in any way more difficult to preserve the competitive basis in commercial dealings, although they are popularly supposed to do so, for the employer profits immensely by having strong, healthy workers, instead of sickly, disspirited ones (on this point see Professor Walker's " Wages Queston," Chapter III.). If however the popular idea is correct, and the factory laws do in fact constitute a hindrance to the competitive system, *to that extent* they are an evil, but an evil that goes to mitigate only to a slight degree the humanitarian benefits secured.

Another object of the factory laws, that of giving opportunity to every child to be equipped with some minimum of education before it enters into the competitive world, is distinctly one which makes the conditions for competition more, and not less perfect. I conclude then that the antagonism between the factory laws and the competitive system is very slight, and that the good that is sought to be obtained, and is obtained by them, is not one that implies a corresponding decline in the force of competition.

As I have already pointed out (pages 92-94), it appears to me to be a mistake to adduce the Post Office as an instance of State Socialism. The State like any other corporation may enter upon commercial enterprises, but if the services it receives and renders in connection with those enterprises are rewarded on a competitive basis, the mere fact that the profits (if any) of the enterprise go into the coffers of the State, do not render them "socialistic,"—not socialistic at any rate in the sense of being opposed to the competitive system. In the case of some departments of the Post Office the example is complicated by the fact that powers of monopoly are taken by the Government, but practically a monopoly is no interference with competition, if by its means services are rendered to the community at a lower rate than they otherwise would be. The salt monopoly that we hear of in India, which enables

the State to exact an exorbitant price for that
necessary of life, does interfere with competition,
and is a true case of State Socialism ; but the
Post Office is merely a case of the community's
trading corporately, and agreeing to a monopoly where a monopoly brings with it extraordinary economy of management ; when it
does *not* bring this, the State sometimes trades
on equal terms with other competitors (as for
instance in the management of its telephones
in England).

The · proposals again for free elementary
schools which are stigmatised as socialistic are
really not so to any important extent. There
may be a touch of communism in the proposal,
but it is not otherwise socialistic. Communism
it is true implies to a certain small extent
Socialism also, for you cannot have a public
distribution of property without deducting in
some measure from the rewards that would

otherwise be allotted by the competitive system
for work and services; and in as far as the
proposed free education would be a discouragement to men to work (to educate their children was formally a stimulus to work—that
stimulus would be removed), it would no
doubt be socialistic, and would so far be an
evil.   But the importance of this danger (which
would probably come but slightly into operation) is in my view altogether outweighed by
the immense benefit of securing a better chance
of at least a start in education for every child,
which would itself be making the antecedent
conditions for competition much more perfect.

My conclusion on this part of my subject is
that competition is the best existing impetus to
useful work, although we hope that it will not
always continue to be so.

But there is another all-important function of
the competitive system which I cannot regard

as likely to be done away with, either by the growth of the moral sense or of intelligence.

This is my second argument against Socialism, and, unlike the first, it may be expected always to remain in force.

II. The competitive system is the only test of whether given work or effort is required by the community or not. It is the only measure of the extent to which it is demanded compared to other work. It is ludicrous to see how much even the experienced are at fault in apprising the value of any new form in which the results of work may be presented, that is to say they have little idea of how much such work is really demanded by, and valued by, the community. It is only the continued "higgling of the market" from day to day, which enables them to tell with exactitude the value of any object. See for example the ignorance, not of the public only, but of the actual owners of whole businesses, as evidenced when they attempt to sell them to the public as joint-stock companies. It is often a matter of most serious debate amongst the proprietors, at what figure they shall fix the nominal price of their share capital; the fact that immediately after the company is launched, the shares are often largely at a discount, or largely at a premium, shows how imperfect is the result of their deliberations; and this, although they may probably have had the advantage of comparing their circumstances with those of others very closely akin. If they had *no* such guides, *how* widely might not their judgment go astray ?

To take another example : an expert in apprising the value of such an article as tea might, if removed from all knowledge of the course of the market for a month or two, be entirely unable to fix a price for a given quality.

My conclusion is, that without the guiding

influence of the competitive system we should
be in the position of a people deprived of all
measures, weights, money, calendars, and clocks;
—of everything in fact that measures value,
or measures things that possess value. With
Shelley's Asia we might sing—

> "And we sail on, away, afar,
> Without a course, without a star."

I am persuaded that in a very short time we
might all of us to a large extent *be devoting
our energies to the wrong things* from sheer
ignorance of what it was that was most needed
by the community. For can we fix how many
cobblers there shall be by ballot? Or will a
plébiscite determine how many musicians the
State shall support? Many of us like music,
still more of us like boots; but the *comparative*
liking of the community for music and boots
will hardly be determined with any success by
a State department,

We must not depend on the *judgment* of men
to determine our financial problems, even if we
can secure that it shall be absolutely disinterested.
I maintain that we are incapable of deciding
what is the *just* wage for a given piece of work
on the merits of the case. For this reason I
believe it to be necessary to maintain the competitive system as a *great pair of scales* in which
to weigh the value of our respective services to
the community.

At any rate before we can safely abolish it
we must be provided with some other measure
of the necessity of any given work, which shall
like this be automatic. This is merely saying
that it is very necessary to know what we are
about ; but knowing what we are about need in
no wise prevent our being generous ; and although I think it most desirable that there
should be retained some means of ascertaining
what the " market value " of a man's work is,

that is no sort of argument against that market value's being exceeded, if it is desirable to pay him more, from motives other than inducing him to undertake the particular piece of work for which he is paid.

IV.

Taking it for granted that the ill effects resulting from the imperfect working of the competitive system, consequent on the faulty nature of its environment and on various disturbing causes (considered in Chapter II.) co-existent with it, are not likely immediately, or perhaps ever, entirely to be removed or reformed, what courses of action are desirable as tending to do away with such ill effects ?

First, I would place a measure of self-denial with regard to luxuries.

Objects of attainment are *luxurious* in inverse proportion to the need for them from the point of view of the physical, mental, æsthetic, and moral welfare of the individual. Of the amount of trouble an object gives in its attainment we have, in spite of the existence of non-competing groups of labour and many other modifying circumstances, our nearest approach to a guide, in its *price*. If when we spend £1 we say to ourselves that we are giving someone or other twenty times as much trouble as when we are spending 1s., we shall in all probability be near the truth.

As to the *need* for any object there is no such test; that must be left to the judgment and conscience of the individual.

If we cease doing any work for the community we necessarily absorb the results of work without doing anything to replace it. *Leisure* is therefore pre-eminently to be classed amongst luxuries.

We have to consider why self-denial with regard to luxuries tends to make the distribution of wealth more equal.

The main point is that my consuming less

gives me the power of allowing others to consume more.

But the precise way in which this fairly obvious principle works out in the practical dealings of life, is one of the most difficult points we have to consider, and has been terribly obscured by the circumstance that many of the most eminent economists have followed a theory which is now no longer accepted. This theory adopted amongst others by Mill, Fawcett, and Cairnes, rests in the first place on the supposition that there is a "wage fund." A right understanding of the theory of wages is of the very utmost importance, but to discuss it here would load my main argument with a long digression. We should moreover be leaving our subject of the connection of ethics and economics for a department of pure economics. The exposition of the subject long received as orthodox in this country, and possibly not quite without authority even yet, is set forth by Mill in his " Political Economy," Book II., Chapter XI., § 1. (See also Cairnes' " Principles of Political Economy," Part II., Chapter I., § 5.)

Prof. F. A. Walker in his book on the "Wages Question," and in his "Political Economy," and Prof. Sidgwick in his " Political Economy," perhaps more completely than their predecessors amongst the opponents of the theory, demonstrate that it is untenable, because more efficient labour by the very fact of its greater efficiency creates an additional fund out of which it will be recouped; that, in fact, "there is no wage-fund irre-"spective of the number and industrial "quality of labourers." (See Prof. F. A. Walker's " Political Economy," Part VI., Chapter VI., § 404, and Prof. H. Sidgwick's luminous chapter on " General Wages," in his

" Principles of Political Economy," Book II.,
Chapter VIII.)

It may be thought that anxious as I am to
urge that luxuries shall not recklessly be in-
dulged in, I have, in disowning the arguments
of Mill, Cairnes, and others which were also
directed to that end, recklessly cut myself adrift
from my best friends. That may be so.
Certainly if we could believe that every time A.
gave a dinner party, not only had he so much
the less to spend in charity, but he also to a
slight extent diminished the wages of every
wage-earner in the country, we should be
furnished with two strong arguments instead of
with one for the cause I am urging. It would
however suppose an effect from the philanthropic point of view out of proportion to the
cause; it would assert that by not eating his
cake he would be able to give it away and
nevertheless have it in hand.

The first and main reason for limiting expenditure in luxuries is I believe that it increases our ability to carry out the ethical duties requiring expenditure of wealth which have been detailed in the course of these papers; notably these lettered *b.* and *c.* in the first chapter (page 43), the provision of health and the provision of education for those who would otherwise be crippled for the want of them.

But, then, as to that part of wealth which we do *not* spend altruistically, is there any ethical choice whether we spend it luxuriously or not? Is it for instance more virtuous to invest than to squander?

Properly speaking, investing money means that it is *not* spent, the spending of it is postponed. In many cases without doubt this postponement is (contrasted with luxurious living) very desirable; for it may be that in the course of time the individual may himself be in real want, and if he had not saved money he would become a burden on some whose money was fully occupied in some non-luxurious expenditure.

Or again, and this is a more frequent case, at his death it may become distributed amongst many, some of whom will expend it non-luxuriously, or the individual may himself at some future date spend on non-luxurious expenditure for others what would in the former case have been spent on luxuries for himself.

With all these chances of its being turned into a less luxurious channel, we should certainly view with satisfaction the postponement of luxurious expenditure (the extreme form of which may be called squandering) in favour of an investment of wealth.

But suppose it happens that all these chances fail. We may even suppose that a thrifty father invests money, and that it is inherited after some years by his son, who sells his investments, and squanders the proceeds. Is there any difference in the result from that which would have come about if the father had squandered the wealth in the first instance? The only difference is the use made of the wealth in the meantime. This to those who believed in a wages fund was very important. But with the overthrow of that theory its importance almost disappears. The effect that actually would be produced would I think be a slight increase in the capital of the country, resulting in a tendency to diminish the current rate of interest, which in turn would tend to diminish the cost of commodities.

But even if the sum in question were a very large one, the effect produced on the rate of interest would be almost infinitesimal. The rate of interest in this country is somewhere about 3 per cent. (if we eliminate insurance against risk of loss of capital) ; it would require an enormous addition to the capital of the country to depress the rate of interest, say ¼ per cent., and the fact that capitalists could supply their business with the necessary capital at ¼ per cent. less interest would only affect the price of the commodities produced by them to a very small fraction of that amount.   Even this slight ,advantage would be temporary, not permanent ; it would last only to the point when the son withdrew the wealth for his own purposes.

Another effect probably of more importance would take place where the conditions were such that an increase of capital would result in a more than proportionate increase in the result of production.   Such conditions would generally be found in new countries.

Prof. Sidgwick summarises the matter in his

" Political Economy," Book II., Chapter VIII.
§ 4: "We should not regard each addition to the
" total stock of capital in the country as contain-
" ing an addition to the wages fund ; but only
"as tending to increase wages indirectly so far
" as it (1) increases aggregate produce by sup-
" plying industry with additional instruments,
" and (2) increases the labourers' share of pro-
" duce, in consequence of the lower rate of inte-
" rest obtained on the increased supply of capi-
" tal." If then a man arranges for the investment
of say £1000 in perpetuity, it will tend only to
an infinitesimally small extent to cheapen all
commodities demanded by the community. If
he squanders the yearly interest accruing from
the £1000, he acts towards the community
hardly at all differently from what he would
have done if, in the first instance, he had
squandered £1000 ; unless indeed it be a
community inadequately provided with capital,

in which case what is paid to him in interest (which he squanders) does not represent *all* the annual benefit to the community accruing from the employment of the additional £1000 in its industry.

My conclusions then on this part of the subject are fairly simple and not far removed from those which have vulgar acceptance. A man if he spends his money luxuriously, gives employment to labour just as much as if he invests it in a railway. In neither case is he acting altruistically. In the one case he parts with his money but receives luxuries; in the other case he temporarily parts with his money, but at the end of a given period receives back a larger amount. In each case the men employed receive wages, but they are under no obligation on this head; they give a due return of work. We can spend money on ourselves, or we can spend it altruistically; we cannot, as

Mill, Cairnes, and Fawcett seem to suppose, do *both*. If we invest money, although we are not immediately spending it on ourselves, neither are we spending it altruistically. At a future time we shall again have the choice of whether we shall spend a larger amount on ourselves or altruistically.

From the necessities of the case the more luxurious our expenditure the smaller is the proportion likely to be that is altruistic. Hence the reason for putting some bounds to luxury— but that is only the first step; the second step is to complete the process by spending altruistically. Investment is good up to a certain point as securing ourselves and those dependent on us against the danger of becoming burdensome to others. After that point there is no particular merit or demerit in investment, it is equivalent simply to postponement of action.

There are other considerations which urge to

self-denial in regard to luxuries, some of which
are set forth almost eloquently in the last
chapter of a booklet in this series called "England's Ideal," by Mr. Edward Carpenter. The
economic premises on which the author builds
many of his conclusions are socialistic, and
consequently as I believe fallacious, but he
has insight and sympathy, and such a sentence
as the following deserves thought:—" Only by
" living simply, that is on a level of simplicity
" at least equal to that of the mass of the people,
" is it possible to know the people, to become
" friends with them, to gauge their wants, &c."

Before trying to realise the ethical effect of
different courses of conduct, it is important to
be accurate in defining to ourselves what that
conduct is. For instance, we must satisfy ourselves as to whether in a particular instance
we are or are not *spending* money. If we
are, whether our spending is productive or

unproductive ; and if the latter, whether it is justified or wasteful unproductive expenditure.

A careful examination of such points as these will show that popular censure or approval often rests on a weak foundation. I will illustrate my meaning by taking two or three concrete examples.

A man papered his study with Government bank-notes. His action was generally esteemed a most flagrant example not only of spending the money and spending it unproductively, but of wasting it. In reality it is very doubtful whether it was any one of the three. The bank-notes were of the nature of receipts from Government for money deposited with it ; by destroying these receipts he consented to forego the debts from Government to himself,—that was all. It is very doubtful whether such cancelment of debts can be called spending money, and certainly it is not spending it unproductively, or wasting it.

Had the man made a present of the bank-notes to the nation for the purpose of reducing the national debt, he would have been overwhelmed with popular gratitude instead of reproach, yet the economic effect of his action would have been much the same.

Similarly, losing money at gambling can hardly be considered spending it; it is more of the nature of a transfer of property (like a gift). It is the winner, not the loser at the gambling-table, who frequently *wastes* the money in unproductive expenditure of useless and mischievous kinds. (There are, of course, other objections to gambling,—such as leaving to chance the distribution of wealth, which ought to be the subject of careful thought with a due sense of responsibility.[1])

[1] Professor Marshall (" Principles of Economics," Vol. I.,

Riding in a first-class railway carriage on the other hand is certainly spending money, and it is usually spending it (as compared with third-class travelling) unproductively. It is conceivable however that the extra comfort may make travelling so much less tiring to a man (or still more likely to a woman) that on arriving at the journey's end, he (or she) would be able to do valuable work that would otherwise be impossible. If the work thus rendered possible were of more value than the extra trouble engendered by travelling first-class, the first-class fare would be productive expenditure.

page 180, foot-note) points out, however, that "gambling "involves an economic loss, even when conducted on "perfectly fair and even terms," for as "the utility to any-"one of an additional £1 diminishes with the number of "pounds he already has," an addition of £100 to the amount of a gambler's holdings will be less of an advantage than a deduction of £100 will be a disadvantage; it follows then that on an (monetarily) even bet the expectation of disadvantage is greater than that of advantage.

K

I believe this case to be rare. The example presents some other interesting features. It is conceivable that carrying a passenger first-class at 3d. a mile might pay the railway companies better than carrying a passenger third-class at 1d. a mile. In such a case some part of the extra fare paid by the first-class passenger would go to pay for the extra trouble involved by his luxury; but some part of it would go to help the railway company to provide cheap travelling for the third-class community. It is an idea of this sort I believe which is at the bottom of the popular notion that it is " mean " of a man who can afford to travel first-class, to travel third. But curiously enough the facts are all the other way. £1000 received in third-class fares puts more profits in the railway companies' pockets than £1000 received in first-class fares; the first-class travellers, so far from paying some of the third-class travellers' fares, are actually themselves helped to pay their fares by the third-class travellers. Nor is this surprising when we consider that on the average there are nearly twice as many seats in a third-class coach (containing say six compartments with five seats a side) as in a first-class coach (containing say four compartments with four seats a side).

Mr. George Findlay, general manager of the L. & N. W. R., in a report submitted to the International Railway Congress at Paris (September, 1889) says:—" The railway companies " have spent and are spending large sums of " money in providing the most luxurious accom-"modation, and every facility and convenience for " the benefit of the superior classes, but they are " doing this practically at their own expense, " *and it is really the humble and once despised* " *third-class traveller who furnishes the sinews* " *of war.*" Meanness then evidently does not come into the case. [In some cases of course the circumstances are reversed. Thus the managers of theatres could not, generally speaking (with equally expensive performances), have 1s. or 6d. galleries, if they had no dress circles.] Returning to railway travelling, my conclusion is that first, as opposed to third-class railway travelling is in the vast majority of cases unproductive expenditure, and when I further consider in how many cases, were it not for the existence of false ideas, the first-class travellers themselves would get more pleasure by having the money representing the excess fares to spend in other ways, I am compelled also to think that it is often *wasteful* expenditure.

In money wisely spent in the encouragement of art we have on the other hand an example of unproductive expenditure as free as it is possible to be from the reproach of being *wasted*, if we have regard to the higher forms of present and future happiness.

In attempting to answer the question which heads this chapter, the first recommendation which we have to consider is the placing on oneself of a certain measure of self-restraint with regard to the luxuries of life.

Second, I would place discouragement of a disproportionate love of possession. Possibly the distinction between this and the first recommendation is not very marked. The man who prides himself on being the possessor of half a county is in a way enjoying a form of luxury. Anyway the reasons against lust of possession are very similar to those against lust of luxury, with the addition that when wealth exceeds a certain amount we have to bear in mind the likelihood of mismanagement, and the evils of management by agents. A certain minimum of possession is necessary to life ; a good deal

beyond this minimum is necessary to develope
life to its full capacities and to minister to its
happiness and pleasure.   Possession then,
even luxurious possession, is in itself a good
thing.   The important thing to recognise is,
that it is not a good to be enjoyed at the
expense of others, not even a good to be
enjoyed with much satisfaction whilst others
are lacking it, but emphatically one to be enjoyed *in conjunction* with them.

Thirdly, I would plead for recognition of the
principle that responsibility towards others is
involved in the way in which we regulate our
own money affairs.   The advocate of a moral
life does not confine his arguments to a consideration of how conduct will affect the individual; he lays stress on the effects on others.
We are all concerned in that important field of
conduct which has to do with monetary dealings;
for we are all buyers, and most of us sellers of

something or other, and it is difficult to see why a part of our daily life so universal in its import, should be excluded from consideration by the moralist.

The only supposition that makes such exclusion reasonable is that self-interest is universally dominant, and that a pursuance of self-interest by each is synonymous with the interest of the whole community. Even the brief treatment received by some of the tangled questions of enconomics in these papers has been enough to show how completely this principle lacks in sufficiency as a guide to conduct. Only of the competitive system could it be supposed for a moment to be true, and we have seen how numerous and how important are the economic factors in modern, commercial, and industrial problems which are entirely distinct from the competitive system ; but even when competition is perfect (and how very excep-

tional it is to find any approach to perfect competition!) we have discovered ample reasons
for laying aside *laissez faire*, and have found
for the individual a large field for ethical action.

We have touched for example on the question of investments, and we concluded that it
was not right to invest in immoral or even in
useless trades.   But let us pursue the question
somewhat further.   What shall we say about
risky investments?   Here at anyrate it might
be supposed that the interest of the individual
was synonymous with that of the community.
The successful floating of a bogus company
rewards rascality; the community suffers by the
encouragement of dishonesty in its midst, but
so do those who have invested their money.
But suppose a man to have twenty investments
which, taken together, pay well, but amongst
which one turns out to be fraudulent.   An ade-
quate investigation of the affairs of the twenty

companies might be so much trouble to him as to cost more than the loss sustained on the one bad investment. His ventures have paid on the average, and he has on the whole acted in accordance with what his own interests would dictate, but by so doing he has acted *contrary* to the interests of the community, for one-twentieth of his invested capital has been employed in the direct remuneration of fraud. I am not maintaining that no investments into which an element even of considerable risk enters, are legitimate.

But risks arise from various causes. There may be a risk of dishonesty in the promoters of a concern; this arises from lack of investigation of their characters. There may be a risk of market fluctuations which will affect commercial enterprises; this may be diminished or increased by availing ourselves or not, of the existing information concerning the conditions likely to affect the market in question. Or again, suppose that a mechanical invention is to be tested, there is a risk of failure; in this case the risk of investment may be diminished by an investigation of the invention itself, and the conditions under which it is to do its work.

Now, in the last two examples at any rate, if no one was prepared to run any risk, industry and enterprise would be confined within narrow limits, for *some* risk is not to be eliminated.

But the risk of injury to the community is not always the same as that to the individual. For instance, we may imagine an individual having three investments the riskiness of which are respectively of the three kinds set forth above. We will suppose that the risk to him is in each case ten to one in favour of its turning out well. If one of the investments turns out badly, to him it matters not which it is, but to the community it matters very much; in the second and third instances a failure of the investment will merely mean that energy has been spent in vain; in the first instance it will mean that dishonesty has been encouraged. Taking this matter of investment as an example then, we see that the conduct dictated by purely economic considerations may be modified by ethical considerations; and this establishes the principle of responsibility towards others in the way we regulate our own money affairs.

Fourthly, let us combat the social power of wealth. Mr. Herbert Spencer, in endeavouring to ascertain the root-cause of commercial immorality, attributes it in the first place to the greed for wealth, and the greed for wealth he believes to be immediately consequent on the worship paid to those who are wealthy and nothing but wealthy, by those who are less so. The remedy he advocates is for no respect to be paid to wealth *as* wealth; and we might further urge that the wealthy should not value or hold as of any account respect or worship (for in many cases it almost amounts to worship) received by them on account of their position.

Mr. Spencer puts the case so forcibly that it is worth while to quote part of what he says:—

" The great inciter of these trade mal-" practices is intense desire for wealth, and if " we ask why this intense desire? the reply is—" it results from the *indiscriminate respect paid* " *to wealth.*

" To be distinguished from the common " herd, to be somebody, to make a name, a " position, this is the universal ambition." . . . " On entering the world, the lessons that may " have been taught about the nobility of self-" sacrifice, the reverence due to genuine merit, " the admirableness of high integrity are quickly " neutralised by experience ; men's actions

" proving that these are not their standards of
" respect. It is soon perceived that while
" abundant outward marks of deference from
" fellow-citizens may almost certainly be gained
" by directing every energy to the accumulation
" of property, they are but rarely to be gained
" in any other way; and that even in the few
" cases where they are otherwise gained, they
" are not given with entire unreserve, but are
" commonly joined with a more or less manifest
" display of patronage." . . . .

" From early childhood the sayings and
" doings of all around " . . . " have generated
" the idea that wealth and respectability are
" two sides of the same thing. This idea,
" growing with their growth, and strengthening
" with their strength, becomes at last almost
" what we may call an organic conviction, and
" this organic conviction it is which prompts
" the expenditure of all their energies in money

"making.   We contend that the chief stimulus
"is not the desire for wealth itself, but for
"the applause and position which the wealth
"brings." . . .

    " It is incredible that men should make the
"sacrifices, mental and bodily, which they do,
"merely to get the material benefits which
"money purchases," . . "but," . . "if the
"desire for that homage which wealth brings
"is the chief stimulus to their strivings after
"wealth, then is the giving of this homage
"(when given, as it is, with but little discrimi-
"nation) the chief cause of the dishonesties
"into which these strivings betray mercantile
"men."

    . . . . . . To the evil "every draw-
"ing-room furnishes nourishment in the ad-
"miration awarded to costliness; to silks that
"are 'rich,' that is, expensive; to dresses that
"contain an enormous quantity of material,

" that is, are expensive ; to laces that are hand-
" made, that is, expensive ; to diamonds that are
" rare, that is, expensive ; to china that is old,
" that is, expensive ; and from scores of small
" remarks and minutiæ of behaviour, which, in
" all circles, hourly imply how completely the
" idea of respectability involves that of costly
" externals, there is drawn fresh pabulum."

" We are all implicated. We all, whether
" with self-approbation or not, give expression
" to the established feeling. Even he who dis-
" approves this feeling, finds himself unable to
" treat virtue in threadbare apparel with a
" cordiality as great as that which he would
" show to the same virtue endowed with pros-
" perity. Scarcely a man is to be found who
" would not behave with more civility to a
" knave in broadcloth than to a knave in
" fustian." . . . . .

" Hence then, is it that men persevere in

"these evil practices which all condemn. They
"can purchase a homage which, if not genuine,
"is yet, so far as appearances go, as good as the
"best."

But Mr. Spencer's argument reaches further
than the question of commercial immorality;
that is not the only evil generated by an undue
desire for wealth; is it not evident that in
almost every detail we have considered, both a
more equal and a m.re equitable distribution of
wealth would be greatly facilitated if there were
less wealth-love? And if a main cause of love
of wealth-accumulation is wealth-worship, then
the principle of discountenancing such worship
requires little recommendation.

One of the great difficulties in following this
principle is the very fact that on the way in
which men spend wealth greatly depends the
well-being of their fellows; hence the strong
tendency to *conciliate* wealthy men, so that

they may use their power in desired ways.   It
is certainly very natural that the inhabitants of
a town who may possibly be benefited by
being provided with a park or a free library, or
who may or may not have their leases renewed
on favourable terms, shall treat the Duke, who
has estates in the neighbourhood, with exceptional politeness; and certainly so long as there
is no such conscious palliation of demerit as
Mr. Spencer contemplates, and further, so
long as there is nothing toadying, or undignified,
or lacking in self-respect, or of the nature of
flattery, in the conduct of the townsmen, I
should by no means wish to see them less polite.
It is not the politeness, but the *exceptionalness*
of the politeness received, that gives wealthy
men a feeling of self-satisfaction which acts as
an unduly powerful stimulus on them to remain
wealthy, and to become more wealthy.   It is
one way (and to many the easiest) of satisfying

L

the craving for individual distinction. Obviously the best way to meet the matter is to prevent the distinction's being exceptional, to treat everyone alike with politeness and respect whether rich or poor. By this I do not of course mean that we should make it a rule to address our office boy as "Tommy Robinson, Esq.," or that we should salute our cook in precisely the same way as we should salute the Lord Chief-Justice. The *formalities* of life are not of great importance or what influence a man's self-respect. It is something deeper than these. Real kindness and personal and respectful feeling are the sorts of politeness we must try and equalise between rich and poor. To do away with some of the distinctions in formalities may also be desirable and help in the same direction, but we must give heed that in doing so we do not outstrip ourselves. The essence of politeness to another is found in adding to his mental comfort, to his ease. An equality of form will not have this effect if there is on either side a feeling of anything *forced* or artificial.

Lastly, I would urge that in the application of the principle advocated in these papers, that namely of applying ethical considerations to economic problems, and bringing ethical tests to bear where matters of economic conduct come in question, generosity and discrimination should go hand in hand. I have endeavoured to show that on the whole competition is a good friend to us, and that the worst evils of which we have to complain exist where the competitive system is in imperfect operation, or is not in operation at all. But we must beware of narrow applications of conclusions which may in the main be sound. For example, it may be objected that profit-sharing with workmen, unless an immediate commercial return is seen, is likely to work injuriously, for it is "opposed to the competitive system;" but we have had considerations of a sufficiently varied character brought before us to show us that we must not so summarily dispose of economic questions. Suppose a case in which profit-sharing is carried on to a larger extent than the increased returns from industry induced thereby justify; so far it is true there is a direct and immediate influence opposed to competition. But suppose it can further be shown that such profit-sharing induces providence, which in the long run results in higher intelligence and education; we are at once furnished with the most powerful battering-ram to level to the ground those walls of division between various groups of industry, which Cairnes points out render them practically uncompeting. So that, taking a larger area into our field of vision, it may be that we find the ultimate and lasting result of profit-sharing (even of that which in the first instance exceeds the surplus results consequent on improved efficiency and industry), to be a powerful aid to the realisation of true and · perfect competition.

If our action is not to be random and confused we must formulate our thought, but in the application of formulated thought imagination and generosity must be ever with us; imagination to prevent our view's being confined when it ought to be wide, and generosity to keep us safe from petty or pedantic enforcement of the principles of conduct we may have evolved.

Taking a wider field of morals into consideration, I would not wish to exaggerate the importance of the present inquiry; it is limited by the effect on human happiness of economic matters, and though the particular way in which wealth is distributed has an important bearing thereon, there are many other things besides, which minister to happiness, such as health, strength, . intellect, culture, and morality. Ill-tempered rich people may of course be much less happy than good-tempered poor ones. Indeed, the importance of the subject of the distribution of wealth consists chiefly in the fact that its bene- ficial accomplishment is often antecedent to other elements of happiness; to a greater extent than they, is it a means to happiness rather than the end accomplished. But we must nevertheless remember that unless this means takes effect to some considerable extent, the other agents of happiness may be rendered entirely inoperative. The basis of happiness is ordinarily material, though the superstructure may not be so. The arts have no charm for one gnawed by real pangs of hunger.

Shortly I do not suggest that ethics be confined to the field of economics, I merely urge their extension thereto.

THE END.

Cowan & Co., Limited, Printers, Perth.

www.ingramcontent.com/pod-product-compliance
Lightning Source LLC
Chambersburg PA
CBHW030846270326
41928CB00007B/1237